Micro-simulating child poverty in 2010 and 2020

Mike Brewer

James Browne

Robert Joyce

Holly Sutherland

Institute for Fiscal Studies

Copy-edited by Anne Rickard

The Institute for Fiscal Studies
7 Ridgmount Street
London WC1E 7AE

Published by

The Institute for Fiscal Studies
7 Ridgmount Street
London WC1E 7AE
Tel: +44 (0)20 7291 4800
Fax: +44 (0)20 7323 4780
Email: mailbox@ifs.org.uk
Website: http://www.ifs.org.uk

Printed by

Patersons, Tunbridge Wells

ISBN: 978-1-903274-59-0

Preface

The Joseph Rowntree Foundation has supported this project as part of its programme of research and innovative development projects, which it hopes will be of value to policy makers, practitioners and service users. The facts presented and views expressed in this report are, however, those of the authors and not necessarily those of the Foundation. Neither are the views expressed necessarily those of the other individuals or institutions mentioned here, including the Institute for Fiscal Studies, which has no corporate view. The authors are grateful to Helen Barnard, who managed the project at JRF, and to Robert Chote, Donald Hirsch, Luke Sibieta and various officials at HM Treasury, the Department for Work and Pensions and the Child Poverty Unit who offered comments on drafts and advice on methods.

Mike Brewer, James Browne and Robert Joyce are at the Institute for Fiscal Studies, and Professor Holly Sutherland is at the Institute for Economic and Social Research, University of Essex. Correspondence to: m.brewer@ifs.org.uk.

Contents

Executive summary   **1**

1.   Introduction   **3**

2.   Child poverty in the UK: progress to date and targets for the future   **5**

3.   **Child poverty in 2010–11**   **7**
    3.1   Simulating the level of child poverty in 2006–07: a robustness check   7
    3.2   Simulating the level of child poverty in 2010–11   11
    3.3   Packages to meet the child poverty target for 2010   20

4.   **Child poverty in 2020–21**   **29**
    4.1   Simulating the level of child poverty in 2020–21   29
    4.2   Packages to meet the child poverty target for 2020   32

5.   Sensitivities   **35**

6.   Conclusions   **37**

Appendices   **39**
    Appendix 1   Methodology   39
    Appendix 2   Tables of our assumptions / procedures   47
    Appendix 3   Supplementary results   51

References   **56**

Executive summary

The 2008 Pre-Budget Report (PBR) said that 'the Government will take stock of progress towards its 2010 and 2020 child poverty target in the [2009] Budget'.[1] As background to that exercise, this paper updates our previous analysis of the prospects for child poverty in the UK in 2010–11 and 2020–21.

The government has a target of halving the number of children in poverty from 3.4 million in 1998–99 to 1.7 million in 2010–11 (where being in poverty is defined as living in a household with less than 60% of median income, measured Before Housing Costs (BHC)). The number of children in poverty stood at 2.9 million in 2006–07.

Our central forecast is that child poverty will fall by more than half a million between 2006–07 and 2010–11, to around 2.3 million. This reflects: benefit and tax credit increases that have been announced by the government, but not yet implemented; the slowdown in the economy from 2008 to 2009; and the likely real rise in most means-tested benefits and tax credits in April 2010 if inflation is forecast to be negative.

This would mean that child poverty had fallen by around a third between 1998–99 and 2010–11, but that it would remain 600,000 higher than the government's target.

There are many uncertainties around this forecast, two of which have been quantified:

First, our forecast for child poverty in 2010 would be slightly higher if we took account of the fact that the survey used to measure household incomes seems to under-record incomes of some low-income families with children.

Second, our forecast of child poverty in 2010 would be very slightly lower if the economy were to perform worse than the Treasury assumed in the Pre-Budget Report. This is because lower employment and real earnings have more effect on median income (and thus the poverty line) than on the income of low-income families with children (in which the parents are less likely to be working than in the median household). However, the measure of poverty that combines relative income with material deprivation is forecast to increase if there is a deep recession.

Of the possible policy packages that we analyse, increasing the per-child element of the Child Tax Credit (CTC) by about 30% on top of the uprating already planned would hit the 2010 child poverty target at the lowest cost – around £4.2 billion. This would increase the number of working parents facing very high marginal effective tax rates, and the incentive to work at all would be weakened for the second worker in a couple. These feedback effects – which would increase child poverty or increase the cost to the government of meeting its target – are not reflected in our modelling.

Whether or not this Child Tax Credit package was implemented, child poverty would remain a long way above target in 2020 if the usual uprating rules were followed between 2010 and 2020. Increases in benefits and tax credits for low-income families with children would not keep pace with increases in median income.

---

[1] Para 5.13 in HM Treasury (2008) [PBR].

Of the tax and benefit packages we looked at, the only policy generous enough to enable child poverty to fall to 5% by 2020 would cost around £37 billion, and this is without accounting for non-reporting of benefit and tax credit income in the survey with which child poverty is officially measured and by assuming that non-take-up of tax credits and benefits halves. This package involves uprating Income Support (IS) payments for parents and the per-child element of the Child Tax Credit by 5.5% per year in real terms between 2010 and 2020; increasing all other tax credits and benefits for parents in line with earnings between 2010 and 2020; raising the Working Tax Credit for couples with children by 60% after it has been earnings-uprated between 2010 and 2020; and uprating all benefits and tax credits for non-parents in line with prices between 2010 and 2020.

Just as this report was being finalised, the government suggested that a child poverty rate of 10% might be consistent with meeting its 2020 target. Even assuming that the government implemented the package thought to be sufficient to hit the 2010 target, it would need to do considerably more to bring child poverty down from 13% in 2010 to 10% in 2020. Increasing all benefits and tax credits in line with earnings, for example, would cost £12 billion a year but leave child poverty roughly constant; spending £30 billion a year would put child poverty comfortably below 10%.

Our forecasts of child poverty were produced using a static micro-simulation model, augmented with projects of key demographic characteristics that affect the income distribution. This paper supersedes our previous estimates by using more recent data on household incomes, economic and demographic projections for 2010 and 2020 and data on benefit and tax credit take-up rates. We have also introduced two adjustments to align our simulation more closely with the survey with which child poverty is officially measured. The net result is that our central forecast of child poverty in 2010–11 under current policies has fallen slightly. On the other hand, our estimate of what it would cost to meet the target in 2010–11 has risen because the children in poverty in 2010–11 are now thought to be further below the poverty line, on average.

1. Introduction

This paper provides an update of our previous assessment (hereafter referred to as BBS) of the prospects for child poverty in 2010 and 2020 under current government policies, and looks at the impact on child poverty of various tax and benefit policies that could be implemented.[2]

In principle, forecasting houschold incomes 12 years into the future can be done using dynamic simulation models, or other models that explicitly 'age' a sample of households observed at the present time. In this paper, though, we use a static micro-simulation model (TAXBEN, which is maintained by the Institute for Fiscal Studies)[3] to project into the future by uprating financial variables and re-weighting our base data on the basis of socio-demographic characteristics. These techniques are regularly used to forecast changes over short periods of time, and here we apply the techniques over longer time horizons.

Since BBS, a number of updates have been released which revised the forecast of child poverty in 2010–11 to take account of policy announcements in Budgets and Pre-Budget Reports since 2006, but there have been no updates to the data or methods underpinning the forecast. This report presents an entirely new set of forecasts, following the basic methodology as for BBS but updating each element.

The basic methodology is best understood as a number of steps (see Appendix 1 for full details):

1. We first use our base data from 2005 and 2006 to construct an estimate of the population's characteristics in 2010 and 2020 (we call this the 'synthetic population'). This is done by:

    • uprating financial variables (such as pre-transfer incomes) using our projections of various price indices;

    • using re-weighting techniques to adjust for expected socio-demographic changes. We have changed the precise way in which we re-weight the data (see Section A1.3 in Appendix 1).

2. We then use a tax and benefit micro-simulation model (TAXBEN) to estimate entitlement to benefits and tax credits, and liabilities to income tax, council tax and national insurance contributions under hypothetical tax and benefit systems in 2010 and 2020. At this stage, we also adjust incomes to account for non-take-up of benefits and tax credits, and the fact that the survey underpinning the Households Below Average Income (HBAI) series – the Family Resources Survey – appears to under-record income from means-tested benefits and tax credits (see appendix C in Brewer et al., 2008).

---

[2] See Brewer, Browne and Sutherland (2006). 2010 should be understood to mean '2010–11' (and equivalently for 2020), because child poverty is measured using the Family Resources Survey (FRS), a survey which covers financial years.

[3] The most recent, although dated, description of TAXBEN is Giles and McCrae (1995), although the basic structure has not changed in the past 13 years.

3. Finally, we construct a measure of net income that mirrors as far as possible the measure used in HBAI, and we obtain our results using the simulated income distribution.

The most important ways in which the forecasts in BBS have been updated are:

1. We use more recent data on the income and other characteristics of households. We now use the 2005–06 and 2006–07 data from the Family Resources Survey (FRS) as the 'base data' from which we project forward to 2010 and 2020, rather than the 2002–03 and 2003–04 data that were used in BBS.

2. We take account of the considerable recent changes to the macroeconomic outlook in our forecasts for employment, real earnings growth and price indices, which, in general, leads us to assume that real earnings and employment will grow by less between 2006–07 and 2010–11 than assumed in BBS.

3. We use updated demographic projections for 2010–11 and 2020–21.

4. We use the latest data on take-up rates for means-tested benefits and tax credits.

There are a number of things that have been done differently from BBS:

1. We make an adjustment to our simulated poverty lines in 2010–11 and 2020–21 in order to account for the fact that our simulation technique slightly underestimates the level of child poverty that was recorded in 2006–07.

2. As a variant, we introduce an adjustment to our simulated receipt of benefits and tax credits to take account of the fact that the FRS (the survey that is used officially to measure child poverty) seems to record lower receipt of benefits and tax credits than implied by administrative data.

3. We do not include scenarios for lone parent employment in 2010–11 (although we do conduct a crude test of the sensitivity of our results to the 2010 lone parent employment rate), partly because the forecasts in BBS seem to have been too optimistic.

4. For 2020–21, we explore the impact of changes in earnings inequality.

The outline of this paper is as follows. Section 2 gives an overview of child poverty in the UK in the recent past, and outlines the child poverty targets. Section 3 presents our projections for child poverty in 2010 under current policies and analysis of hypothetical policy packages to bring child poverty to target in 2010. Section 4 reports projections for child poverty in 2020 under current policies and looks at the effect of hypothetical uprating policies between 2010 and 2020 on child poverty. Section 5 reports sensitivity tests on our results. Section 6 concludes. More details of our methodology can be found in Appendices 1 and 2. Appendix 3 contains some supplementary results.

2. Child poverty in the UK: progress to date and targets for the future

The government has a target for child poverty in the UK in 2010–11 to be one-half of its 1998–99 level. Progress will be assessed using three definitions of poverty – a relative poverty indicator, an absolute poverty indicator and a material deprivation indicator.[4]

Table 1. Progress towards halving child poverty in the UK by 2010–11

	Relative poverty, UK, modified OECD (BHC)		Absolute poverty, UK, modified OECD (BHC)		Material deprivation	
	%	Million	%	Million	%	Million
1998–99	26.1	3.4	26.1	3.4	20.8	2.6
1999–00	25.7	3.4				
2000–01	23.4	3.1				
2001–02	23.2	3.0				
2002–03	22.6	2.9	14.1	1.8		
2003–04	22.1	2.9	13.7	1.8		
2004–05	21.3	2.7	12.9	1.7	17.1	2.2
2005–06	22.0	2.8	12.7	1.6	16.3	2.1
2006–07	22.3	2.9	13.1	1.7	15.6	2.0
Change since 1998–99	–3.8	–0.6	–13.0	–1.7	–5.2	–0.6
Target for 2010–11		1.7				1.3

Notes: Reported changes may not equal the differences between the corresponding numbers due to rounding. The left-hand panel uses data for the UK and incomes equivalised using the modified OECD equivalence scale. For the purposes of the child poverty target in 2010–11, the Department for Work and Pensions (DWP) has had to estimate the level of relative child poverty in the UK in 1998–99 (Northern Ireland was first included in the official HBAI series in 2002–03) – see HM Treasury (2007a).
Source: Brewer et al. (2008).

Table 1 reviews progress to date on the three measures targeted in 2010–11. IFS researchers have argued that the most binding of the government's three measures will be the pure relative poverty target, which is for child poverty in the UK in 2010–11 to be one-half lower than its level in 1998–99, using a poverty line of 60% of median BHC income and the modified Organisation for Economic Co-operation and Development (OECD) equivalence scale.[5] In 2006–07, the number of children in poverty on this measure was 2.9 million, and this means that child poverty has fallen by 600,000 (to the nearest hundred thousand) in the eight years since 1998–99 and needs to fall by a further

---

[4] Before that, the government had a target for child poverty in Britain in 2004–05 to be one-quarter lower than its 1998–99 level (although child poverty was calculated in a slightly different way from the 2010–11 target). This was originally missed by 100,000 measuring incomes BHC and by 300,000 measuring incomes AHC; subsequent rises in child poverty mean that, as of 2006–07 data, the government is short of its original 2004–05 target by 300,000 measuring incomes BHC or by 500,000 measuring incomes AHC, achieving reductions of only 16% and 12%, respectively, between 1998–99 and 2006–07 (all calculated using the McClements equivalence scale).

[5] See Brewer et al. (2005).

1.2 million in the remaining four years between now and 2010–11 to meet this element of the target. Thus, child poverty would need to fall by an average of 300,000 a year between 2006 and 2010, having fallen by an average of 70,000 a year for the previous eight years.

The target for 2020–21 has not yet been defined. When the government announced the target for 2010–11, it also said that it would be impossible to get the HBAI poverty rate down to zero, because surveys:

> always classify as poor some people with high living standards but transitory low incomes ... [As a result,] success in eradicating child poverty could, then, be interpreted as having a material deprivation child poverty rate that approached zero and being amongst the best in Europe on relative low incomes.[6]

But this is a matter of opinion and political judgement.

The data available when the government made this claim showed that the three countries in Europe with the best record on child poverty (Denmark, Finland and Sweden) had relative child poverty rates of between 5% and 10% in 2001, and so Hirsch (2006) and our previous work took a level of child poverty of 5% in 2010 as consistent with meeting the target. We argued last time that 'it could be argued that achieving a child poverty rate of between 5 and 10 per cent in the UK falls some way short of abolishing child poverty: it is not clear, for example, whether Denmark, Finland and Sweden consider that they have abolished child poverty'.[7] Since then, the government has announced that a Child Poverty Bill, to be published in 2009, will enshrine in law the commitment to eradicate child poverty by 2020.

In a recent consultation on how eradication of child poverty could be defined, the government said: 'the best child poverty rate that has ever been achieved in Europe is 5 per cent, but these figures have not been sustained. Using data from 2007, the best in Europe would equate to a level of 10 per cent' (Child Poverty Unit, 2009, para 51). Partly for this reason, but also appealing to the well-known fact that the living standards of households with the very lowest incomes are higher than those with slightly higher incomes (see, for example, Brewer, Goodman and Leicester, 2006), it proposed that:

> legislation sets a target that by 2020 the percentage of children in relative low income should be between 5–10 per cent and that this should be sustained for the long-term (Child Poverty Unit, 2009, para 54).

Child poverty in the UK has been above 15% in every year since 1982, and above 10% in every year for which we have comparable data (1961 to 2006–07), and so achieving a rate of 5% would be historically unprecedented. However, for the purposes of this report, we continue to use 5% (or below) as the target for the child poverty rate in 2020, though this does not necessarily mean that the authors are recommending this particular rate as being consistent with 'abolishing' child poverty.

The government also proposed that eradication of child poverty would mean having a combined material deprivation and low income measure of zero, and of having no persistent poverty, although the precise definitions of each have not been set out yet.

---

[6] Department for Work and Pensions (2003, p. 20).

[7] Brewer, Browne and Sutherland (2006, p. 17).

3. Child poverty in 2010–11

This section presents our simulations for child poverty in 2010–11, and our estimates of what it might cost to hit the government's target.

However, Section 3.1 first discusses an important methodological point which is new to this update, in which we use our simulation methods to simulate child poverty in 2006–07 and compare this to the level recorded in HBAI. This comparison leads us to implement a correction to the simulated poverty line in 2010–11, and these results are presented in Section 3.2. Section 3.3 then looks at five hypothetical policy packages that could be introduced to bring child poverty close to target by 2010.

It is important to note that the fact that policies are analysed in this paper does not mean that the authors are recommending that such policies be introduced. Furthermore, we do not suggest how the money could be raised to pay for the hypothetical policy packages that we model in this paper. If they were paid for using changes in personal taxes or benefits, or changes in other taxes which eventually affected household incomes, or changes to other areas of public spending which eventually affected household incomes, then these changes might also affect the level of child poverty in 2010–11: we do not consider these effects here.

3.1 Simulating the level of child poverty in 2006–07: a robustness check

As detailed in Appendix 1, the basic methodology is best understood as a number of steps:

1. We first use our base data from 2005–06 and 2006–07 to construct an estimate of the population's characteristics in 2010–11 and 2020–21 (we call this the 'synthetic population'). This is done by:

    - uprating financial variables (such as pre-transfer incomes) using our projections of various price and earnings indices;

    - using re-weighting techniques to adjust for expected socio-demographic changes.

2. We then use a tax and benefit micro-simulation model (TAXBEN) to estimate entitlement to benefits and tax credits, and liabilities to income tax, council tax and national insurance contributions under hypothetical tax and benefit systems in 2010 and 2020. At this stage, we also adjust incomes in one of two ways to account for non-take-up of benefits and tax credits, and the fact that the survey underpinning the HBAI series – the Family Resources Survey – appears to under-record income from means-tested benefits and tax credits: Box 1 describes these adjustments.

3. Finally, we construct a measure of net income that mirrors as far as possible the measure used in HBAI, and we obtain our results using the simulated income distribution.

Box 1. Adjusting simulated net incomes to account for non-take-up or non-reporting of means-tested benefits and tax credits

TAXBEN initially calculates entitlements to means-tested benefits and tax credits under hypothetical tax and benefit systems. However, not everyone who is entitled to benefits or tax credits claims them. Incorrectly assuming full take-up would probably mean that the simulation techniques underestimate the level of child poverty, since it is generally the poor (rather than households around the median) who are eligible to means-tested benefits and tax credits, and so it is the poor who will lose out if not all tax credits and benefits are claimed. BBS therefore allowed for incomplete take-up of means-tested benefits and tax credits by making use of the official estimates of the take-up rates (see Appendix 2 for full details of these take-up rates and references), and we repeat this technique in this report.

However, it is becoming increasingly apparent that estimates based on the FRS of the number of families receiving means-tested benefits and tax credits are considerably lower than estimates based on administrative data. This suggests that there is under-reporting of means-tested benefits and tax credit income in the FRS. If this is the case, then it suggests that the official estimates of poverty are overestimates of the 'real' level of poverty. It also suggests that if our simulation techniques allow for incomplete take-up, but assume that all households correctly report income from means-tested benefits and tax credits in the FRS, then we may still underestimate the level of poverty compared with that derived from the FRS.[8] For this reason, we have a variant that explicitly accounts for the non-reporting of income of tax credits and means-tested benefits. Full details are given in Appendix A1.4, but note that the assumption implicit in this is that the accuracy with which the FRS records means-tested benefit and tax credit receipt remains constant over time.

In our adjustments for non-take-up, we do not take account of the fact that it tends to be those households with small entitlements – households which are generally not the poorest in society – that are less likely to claim tax credits or means-tested benefits. We also ignore any interactions between means-tested benefits and tax credits.

When estimating the costs of hypothetical policy packages, we make use of expenditure take-up rates.

As in our previous work (BBS), this has been done separately for 2010–11 and 2020–21. However, as an additional check on this method, we have also used the same methods to simulate the level of child poverty in 2006–07, and compared this with the official rate measured by HBAI. Table 2 gives this comparison: it shows that our simulations underestimate the level of child poverty measuring incomes BHC by about 300,000 in 2006–07 (although there is a much smaller difference measuring incomes After Housing Costs (AHC)). Note that this difference occurs even though the simulated level of median income (and therefore the poverty line) is very similar to the HBAI-recorded level of median income: this suggests that the simulated data are either understating the number of low-income households with children, or overstating the income of low-income households with children, compared with the actual 2006–07 HBAI data.

---

[8] It is not clear why the FRS underestimates the number of recipients of means-tested benefits or tax credits. It could be because recipients of means-tested benefits or tax credits are less likely to participate in the survey, and that the grossing weights fail to compensate for this form of differential non-response. On the other

NB median income?

Table 2. HBAI-measured and simulated child poverty in 2006–07 (UK)

Data source	Before Housing Costs			After Housing Costs		
	Number in poverty (millions)	Poverty rate (%)	Median income	Number in poverty (millions)	Poverty rate (%)	Median income
HBAI	2.9	22.3	£378	3.9	30.5	£321
Simulated, take-up adjustment	2.6	20.5	£379	3.9	30.3	£326
Simulated, take-up and non-reporting adjustment	2.7	20.6	£377	3.9	30.3	£323

Sources: HBAI figures from Brewer et al. (2008). The rest are the authors' calculations based on FRS 2005–06 and 2006–07 using TAXBEN and assumptions specified in the text.

There are a number of reasons why this difference between the simulated data for 2006–07 and the actual HBAI series for 2006–07 might occur:

1. The simulated population uses information on estimated income tax and NI liabilities (estimated by the tax and benefit simulation model), whereas the actual HBAI series uses the information in the FRS on what income tax and NI has been paid by the FRS respondents. Inaccuracies in estimating income tax and NI liabilities or inaccuracies in the information in the FRS on income tax and NI actually paid will therefore lead to differences between the two estimates.

2. The simulated population uses information on estimated entitlements to means-tested benefits and tax credits (estimated by the tax and benefit simulation model), whereas the actual HBAI series uses the information in the FRS on what means-tested benefits and tax credits have been received by the FRS respondents. However, an adjustment has been made to the simulated population to allow for non-take-up and the non-reporting of means-tested benefits and tax credits. (As described in Appendix 1, the adjustment means that families that do not report receipt of means-tested benefits and tax credits despite apparently being entitled are not allocated means-tested benefits and tax credits in the simulated data.) But any inaccuracies in estimating entitlements to means-tested benefits and tax credits, or inaccuracies in the information in the FRS on the amounts of means-tested benefits and tax credits actually received among those who say that they receive some, will lead to differences between the two estimates.

3. The simulated population uses different grossing weights from the actual HBAI series. This is because the grossing weights for the simulated population are based on a different set of control totals from that used by DWP when producing the grossing weights for the official HBAI series. Ideally, the simulated population should make use of the same set of control totals as used by DWP when producing the grossing weights for the official HBAI series, but credible forecasts for 2010–11 and 2020–21 do not exist for all of these totals, and so the approach taken in this project was to use a set of control totals which was as close as possible to those used by DWP but for

hand, it could be because recipients of means-tested benefits or tax credits are participating in the survey but the survey is not recording the fact that they receive means-tested benefits or tax credits.

which reliable forecasts for 2010–11 and 2020–21 exist. In practice, grossing weights are sensitive to the choice of control totals, and so this means that the grossing weights for 2006–07 for individual households may be slightly different from the official HBAI population.

4. The simulated population for 2006–07 comprises households from both the 2005–06 and 2006–07 FRS. This decision was made in order to provide a larger sample of households with children and thereby increase the reliability of the predictions of child poverty in 2010–11. But it also means that the simulated population for 2006–07 comprises different households from the official HBAI estimates for 2006–07, and this makes it much harder to make a detailed comparison of the simulated data and the actual HBAI data for 2006-07.

However, it is not entirely clear whether we should take account of this discrepancy when simulating child poverty in 2010–11 and 2020–21.

One approach would be to ascribe the difference for 2006–07 to an inaccuracy in the simulated data that has been introduced by some feature of the process used to simulate the population (such as using different control totals when producing the grossing weights). In this case, it would be sensible to account for the discrepancy in 2006–07 when using the same techniques to simulate child poverty in 2010–11. One simple way of doing this is to calibrate the simulated poverty line so that the simulated population has the same number of children in relative poverty as the actual HBAI data set. For example, for our simulated data for 2006–07 to give the same child poverty rate as the actual HBAI data for 2006–07, the poverty line in the simulated income distribution would have to be about 2% higher (or around £4.40 a week). We could then assume that the same adjustment needs to happen to the simulated poverty line in 2010–11 and 2020–21.

Another approach would be to ignore the discrepancy that arises for 2006–07. This is effectively what was done in BBS, where it was not possible to compare directly any simulated data with actual HBAI data. This would be a reasonable approach if it were thought that the discrepancy for 2006–07 was due in some way to the nature of the underlying 2006–07 FRS data (such as a tendency for recipients to understate receipt of tax credits and means-tested benefits) that would not be repeated in the 2010–11 FRS.

The size of the discrepancy in 2006–07 means that whether or not the simulated poverty line is adjusted in 2010–11 and 2020–21 makes a substantial difference to the forecast levels of child poverty, and therefore to the cost of meeting the child poverty targets. When we do not adjust the poverty line, the baseline forecast is an estimate of what our simulated income distribution will show in 2010–11, and the cost of hitting the target is the estimated cost of making our simulated income distribution show that the target has been hit. When we do adjust the poverty line, we contend that the baseline forecast is closer to an estimate of what HBAI will say about child poverty in 2010–11, and the estimated cost of hitting the target is the estimated cost of making HBAI show that the target has been hit. We have therefore decided that the main results for 2010–11 and 2020–21 should make use of this adjustment, but estimates without it are presented in Appendix 3.

3.2 Simulating the level of child poverty in 2010–11

Table 3 shows the predictions of child poverty (and median income growth) in 2010–11 under the policy baseline (see Box 2), the central forecast and the bad recession scenario (see Box 3), using both the take-up adjustment used in BBS and the new adjustment which accounts separately for non-reporting of tax credits and benefits in HBAI. Results are shown for poverty using incomes measured Before and After Housing Costs, although the government's child poverty target is only in relation to income measured Before Housing Costs. Table 3 also includes, for reference, the actual levels of child poverty in 2006–07, the target level of child poverty in 2010–11 and the level of child poverty previously forecast by BBS (updated for subsequent policy announcements).

We also include results using the combined material deprivation and relative income measure of poverty, for which the government has separate targets (shown in Table 3). By this measure, a child is in poverty if they are materially deprived and they live in a household whose equivalised income is less than 70% of the median: see Box 4 for more details.

Box 2. The 2010 policy baseline

The baseline tax and benefit policies are intended to represent a 'no change' policy scenario. We define our baseline by assuming that the usual policies for uprating thresholds and benefits will continue indefinitely, except where the government has already made other commitments and allowed for these in its public finance forecasts. Table A2.2 in Appendix 2 details what we mean by 'usual' uprating policies (a mixture of statutory requirements and the 'usual' practice in recent years).

Box 3. The 'bad recession scenario' for 2010

There has been considerable change in macroeconomic prospects since BBS, and the outlook remains very uncertain in the near term. Recognising this uncertainty, we have modelled the effect on child poverty in 2010–11 of a recession that is somewhat worse than that assumed by HM Treasury (HMT) when producing its public finance forecasts.[9] Specifically, this scenario assumes that the difference between total employment in 2010–11 and the estimated long-run employment level is twice as large as in our central forecast (see Appendix A1.3 for details of how our projected employment totals for 2010–11 were constructed); that real earnings fall by 1% between 2007 and 2010 (instead of staying the same as in our central forecast); and that total nominal GDP growth between 2007 and 2010 is 1% lower than in our central forecast.[10] We call this the 'bad recession scenario'.

---

[9] The government does not publish a forecast of unemployment, despite presumably basing key decisions such as how much money to allocate to Jobcentre Plus on such a forecast, but HM Treasury publishes the assumption about the claimant count that it uses when forecasting the public finances. However it stresses that this number is not a forecast by HM Treasury, but merely a cautious interpretation of estimates made by outside forecasters and commentators.

[10] The nominal GDP assumption is of minor importance, but affects our uprating of income from capital (see Table A2.2). This is effectively an assumption about real GDP since we do not change our inflation assumptions for the bad recession scenario.

Box 4. Forecasting the combined low income and material deprivation indicator

Section 2 said that the government is now tracking three indicators of child poverty, one of which defines a child as poor if they live in a household with less than 70% of the median income and are materially deprived.

We have provided two forecasts of this measure of child poverty. One assumes that the material deprivation score of each family in our simulated 2010–11 data is the same as it was when the family was interviewed (in 2005–06 or 2006–07). This can be thought of as a worst-case scenario. The second predicts the material deprivation score for each family given their simulated income in 2010–11 (more details are in Appendix 1, Section A.1.6). But this should not be thought of as the best-case scenario. Berthoud et al (2004) showed that the relationship between changes in income and changes in material deprivation for individual households is much weaker than that between material deprivation and income when comparing different households. On the other hand, that study also showed that there was an unexplainable decline in material deprivation over time that could not be accounted for by rising incomes. The first of these points would suggest that we have overstated the decline in material deprivation between 2006–07 and 2010–11, but the second would mean that we have understated the decline.

Figure 1. UK lone parent employment, 1997–2007

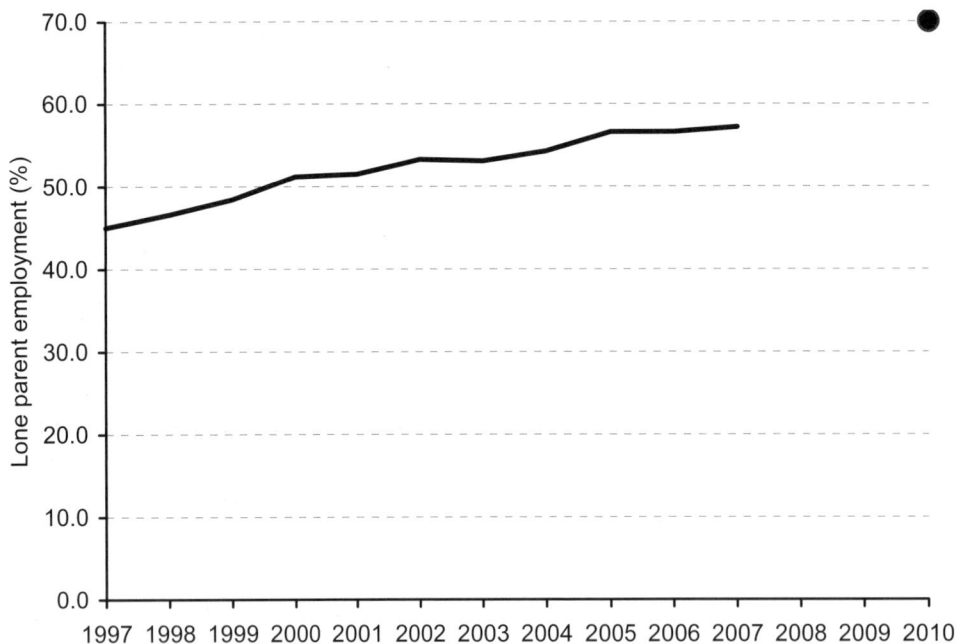

Source: LFS statistics are taken from the DWP 'Opportunity for All' indicator, number 19 (see http://www.dwp.gov.uk/ofa/indicators/indicator-19.asp).

Note that, unlike in BBS, we do not model scenarios for the lone parent employment rate in 2010. Short-term macroeconomic prospects make it less likely that substantial progress can be made in increasing lone parent employment by 2010 – and very unlikely that the rate will reach the government's target of 70% by 2010 – and the lone parent employment rate has recently been roughly flat, as shown in Figure 1. The government has, however, just introduced some welfare-to-work policies that may affect lone parent employment, as well as proposing more changes in the future,[11] so we do include a sensitivity test for the lone parent employment rate in 2010 (see Section 5).

Table 3 shows a number of things:

- Child poverty is forecast to fall from its 2006–07 levels by 2010–11. A large part of this fall can be attributed to measures announced in or since Budget 2007 but whose effect has not yet been seen in actual HBAI figures. But child poverty is still forecast to be higher than the government's target in 2010–11.

- The 'bad recession' scenario slightly lowers child poverty relative to the central forecast. The effect of lower employment and earnings on reducing the median income (and thereby the poverty line) more than offsets any income-reducing effects on low-income households with children; this is unsurprising given that low-income people are on average less dependent on earned income than those in the middle of the income distribution. However, one should not conclude from this that 'bad recessions are good for child poverty': a much more important impact of a bad recession would be to reduce tax revenues and increase some spending on means-tested benefits – something which we have not been able to quantify – which would make it much harder for the government to find extra resources to spend on reducing child poverty. This is very important, given that the bad recession still leaves child poverty well above the target, and therefore still leaves the government needing to finance additional policy packages.

- Given actual real earnings growth between 2006 and 2007, and our assumptions about real earnings growth between 2007 and 2010, the average annual real growth in average earnings between 2006 and 2010 is –0.1% in the central forecast and –0.3% in the bad recession scenario. Average annual growth in real median income between 2006 and 2010 is close to zero under our central forecast, and negative in the 'bad recession' scenario.

- Our new baseline forecast of child poverty in 2010–11 is fairly similar to the one produced in the last update made to BBS: after Budget 2008, IFS researchers estimated that spending of £2.8 billion a year on the Child Tax Credit would be needed to bring the government back on track to meet its target, which corresponded to a projected 2010 child poverty rate of 18.2% under current policies.[12] This means that the net impact of adjusting our simulated poverty line (see Section 3.1), updating the underlying data, updating the employment and earnings forecasts, updating take-up rates, and updating the control totals and generating new grossing weights is to reduce slightly the projected 2010 child poverty rate. Clearly, without the new poverty line adjustment, our projected 2010 child poverty rate would have fallen further (as confirmed by Table A3.1 in Appendix 3).

- Adjusting for non-reporting as well as non-take-up has a very small child poverty-increasing effect under the baseline. This is what we would expect, because not counting non-reported receipt of tax credits and benefits as income means that the

[11] Between 2008 and 2011 the government will lower the age of the youngest child at which a lone parent is no longer eligible for IS as a lone parent from 16 to 7, and had just proposed to pilot measures forcing those whose youngest child is aged between 3 and 6 to undertake activities to get them ready for work.

[12] This assessment was made after Budget 2008, and reported in evidence to the Treasury Select Committee. See Q67 of the oral evidence in House of Commons Treasury Committee (2008).

Table 3. Forecast child poverty in 2010–11 under the policy baseline

Forecast	Before Housing Costs					After Housing Costs		
	Real annual growth in median income, 2006–2010 (%)	Relative low income indicator		Material deprivation and low income indicator		Real annual growth in median income, 2006–2010 (%)	Relative low income indicator	
		Children in poverty (millions)	Child poverty rate (%)	Children in poverty (millions)	Child poverty rate (%)		Children in poverty (millions)	Child poverty rate (%)
Central forecast, 2010–11, take-up adjustment	+0.0	2.3	17.8	1.8	13.7–14.1	–0.0	3.4	26.1
Bad recession scenario, 2010–11, take-up adjustment	–0.5	2.3	17.5	1.7	13.1–13.4	–0.6	3.3	25.7
Central forecast, 2010–11, take-up and non-reporting adjustment	–0.0	2.3	18.0	1.8	13.7–14.0	–0.1	3.4	26.7
Bad recession scenario, 2010–11, take-up and non-reporting adjustment	–0.5	2.3	17.7	1.7	13.0–13.3	–0.6	3.4	26.3
Memo: actual HBAI 2006–07	n/a	2.9	22.3	2.0	15.6	n/a	3.9	30.5
Memo: forecast for 2010–11 based on BBS (GB)	n/a	2.2	18.2	n/a	n/a	n/a	n/a	n/a
Memo: target, 2010–11	n/a	1.7	13.2	1.3	10.4	n/a	n/a	n/a

Notes: All numbers are for UK except the forecast based on BBS, which is for GB. Note that the government's targets are officially in terms of the number of children in poverty, not the rate. Half of the number of children in poverty in 1998–99 is 1.7 million. In our simulated 2010 income distribution, the number of children is 12.9 million, which implies that the poverty rate consistent with the 2010 target is 13.2%. Box 4 explains why a range is given for the material deprivation and relative income measure.

Source: Authors' calculations based on FRS 2005–06 and 2006–07 using TAXBEN and assumptions specified in the text.

increases in benefits and tax credits between 2006 and 2010 reduce measured child poverty by less (see Appendix 1 Section A1.4 for a more comprehensive discussion of the two take-up procedures).

- The combined relative low income and material deprivation measure of poverty shows a small decline between 2006–07 and 2010–11 under the central forecast. The decline is smaller (in absolute and relative terms) than that forecast for the main relative poverty measure, and would leave combined relative low income and material deprivation poverty about 500,000 above the 2010–11 target. The falls that we predict will take place are largely explained by people moving out of relative poverty. Due to the lack of real income growth, relatively few people will move out of material deprivation between 2006 and 2010. Note also that, because real income growth is close to zero, the projected range for child poverty rates under the combined material deprivation/relative income measure is quite small. This is because, with real income growth close to zero, it makes relatively little difference to material deprivation predictions whether or not we assume a relationship between material deprivation and real income.

- The combined material deprivation and relative income measure is projected to show around 200,000 fewer children in poverty in 2010–11 under the bad recession scenario than under the central forecast. This is entirely caused by our prediction (not shown here) that the bad recession would cut the number of children in households with less than 70% of the median income. The number of families experiencing material deprivation alone is predicted to be higher under the bad recession scenario than under the central forecast because the material deprivation component is assumed to be related to absolute levels of income, not relative income.

Figure 2 shows actual rates of child poverty to 2006, and the forecasts for 2010 given in Table 3.

Figure 2. Actual, required and projected path of child poverty, 1998–99 to 2010–11

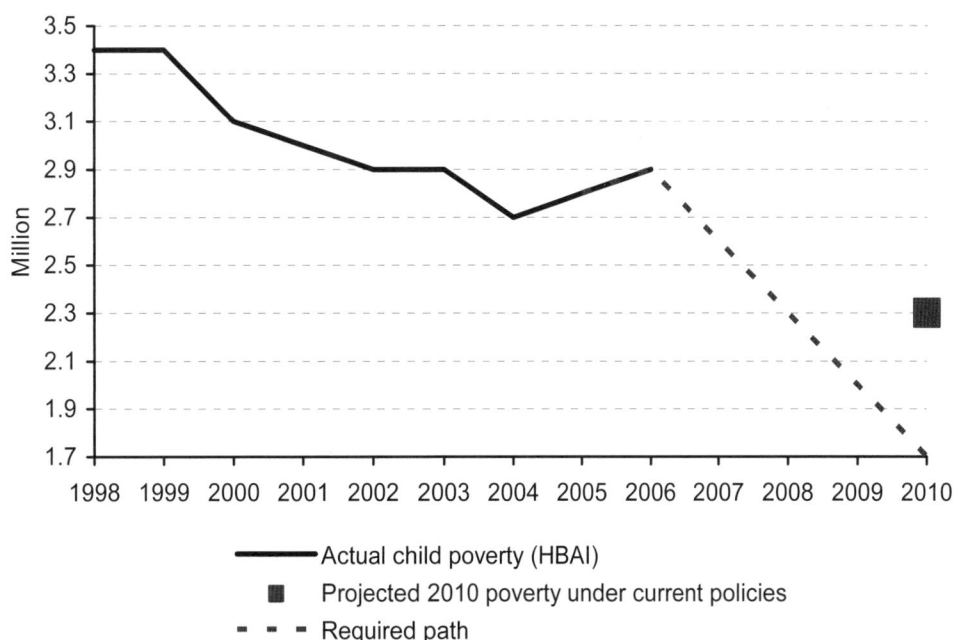

Table 4. Child poverty by family type/employment status in 2010 under the central forecast

	Lone parent		Couple		Workless lone parent		Part-time working lone parent		Full-time working lone parent		Workless couple		One full-time worker couple		Two full-time worker couple		One full-time one part-time couple		Zero full-time and one or two part-time couple		Self-employed couple	
	Number	%	Number	%	Number	%	Number	%	Number	%	Number	%	Number	%	Number	%	Number	%	Number	%	Number	%
2006–7 HBAI	1,156,983	36.5	1,710,430	17.7	929,770	57.5	181,745	19.4	45,584	7.4	436,973	68.1	471,802	20.2	39,116	2.4	91,167	3.2	304,995	46.6	363,361	23.4
2006–7 simulated	1,092,720	34.8	1,566,035	16.1	879,745	54.0	185,170	21.9	27,805	4.2	422,673	58.1	354,889	15.2	23,703	1.3	79,924	3.2	211,963	54.4	472,883	24.7
2010–11 predicted, previous update to BBS	868,812	31.7	1,338,176	14.2	648,433	55.7	198,433	22.4	21,936	3.2	402,230	64.4	337,188	15.0	10,912	0.6	55,561	2.2	216,973	52.9	315,312	18.6
2010–11 predicted, take-up and non-reporting adjustment	942,959	28.6	1,376,653	14.4	785,573	45.0	134,501	15.7	22,885	3.3	413,607	54.2	281,857	11.5	18,526	1.1	64,922	2.7	174,682	44.7	423,059	22.7
2010–11 predicted, take-up adjustment	904,369	27.4	1,390,273	14.5	752,790	43.1	134,563	15.7	17,016	2.5	479,542	62.8	286,809	11.7	10,942	0.6	55,109	2.3	189,650	48.6	368,221	19.7

Table 5. Composition of child poverty count by family type/employment status in 2010 under the central forecast

	Lone parent	Couple	Workless lone parent	Part-time working lone parent	Full-time working lone parent	Workless couple	One full-time worker couple	Two full-time worker couple	One full-time one part-time couple	Zero full-time and one or two part-time couple	Self-employed couple
2006–7 HBAI	40%	60%	32%	6%	2%	15%	16%	1%	3%	11%	13%
2006–7 simulated	41%	59%	33%	7%	1%	16%	13%	1%	3%	8%	18%
2010–11 predicted, previous update to BBS	39%	61%	29%	9%	1%	18%	15%	0%	3%	10%	14%
2010–11 predicted, take-up and non-reporting adjustment	41%	59%	34%	6%	1%	18%	12%	1%	3%	8%	18%
2010–11 predicted, take-up adjustment	39%	61%	33%	6%	1%	21%	12%	0%	2%	8%	16%

Table 6. Child poverty by family type/employment status in 2010 under the bad recession scenario

	Lone parent		Couple		Workless lone parent		Part-time working lone parent		Full-time working lone parent		Workless couple		One full-time worker couple		Two full-time worker couple		One full-time one part-time couple		Zero full-time and one or two part-time couple		Self-employed couple	
	Number	%	Number	%	Number	%	Number	%	Number	%	Number	%	Number	%	Number	%	Number	%	Number	%	Number	%
2006–7 HBAI	1,156,983	36.5	1,710,430	17.7	929,770	57.5	181,745	19.4	45,584	7.4	436,973	68.1	471,802	20.2	39,116	2.4	91,167	3.2	304,995	46.6	363,361	23.4
2006–7 simulated	1,092,720	34.8	1,566,035	16.1	879,745	54.0	185,170	21.9	27,805	4.2	422,673	58.1	354,889	15.2	23,703	1.3	79,924	3.2	211,963	54.4	472,883	24.7
2010–11 predicted, previous update to BBS	868,812	31.7	1,338,176	14.2	648,433	55.7	198,433	22.4	21,936	3.2	402,230	64.4	337,188	15.0	10,912	0.6	55,561	2.2	216,973	52.9	315,312	18.6
2010–11 predicted, take-up and non-reporting adjustment	918,016	27.9	1,367,201	14.3	776,015	42.5	120,303	15.0	21,698	3.3	442,955	52.1	272,325	10.4	15,598	1.0	52,043	2.3	170,966	43.2	413,314	22.5
2010–11 predicted, take-up adjustment	866,095	26.3	1,389,472	14.5	738,199	40.4	111,902	14.0	15,994	2.4	518,133	60.9	277,626	10.6	8,354	0.5	43,892	2.0	181,948	45.9	359,519	19.5

Table 7. Composition of child poverty count by family type/employment status in 2010 under the bad recession scenario

	Lone parent	Couple	Workless lone parent	Part-time working lone parent	Full-time working lone parent	Workless couple	One full-time worker couple	Two full-time worker couple	One full-time one part-time couple	Zero full-time and one or two part-time couple	Self-employed couple
2006–7 HBAI	40%	60%	32%	6%	2%	15%	16%	1%	3%	11%	13%
2006–7 simulated	41%	59%	33%	7%	1%	16%	13%	1%	3%	8%	18%
2010–11 predicted, previous update to BBS	39%	61%	29%	9%	1%	18%	15%	0%	3%	10%	14%
2010–11 predicted, take-up and non-reporting adjustment	40%	60%	34%	5%	1%	19%	12%	1%	2%	7%	18%
2010–11 predicted, take-up adjustment	38%	62%	33%	5%	1%	23%	12%	0%	2%	8%	16%

Tables 4 to 7 give breakdowns of child poverty rates in 2010 by various subgroups (categorised by work status and family type) and the proportion of the total child poverty count that each subgroup comprises, for both the central forecast and the bad recession scenario under the policy baseline. The groups that experience the largest percentage point reductions in the risk of poverty between 2006 and 2010 are workless lone parents, who tend to be close to the poverty line, and workless couples. However, Tables 5 and 7 show that children in poverty are less likely to be in working families in 2010 than in 2006, and therefore more likely to be in workless families (and self-employed couple households). These two results can be explained by the fact that we predict there to be more workless families with children in 2010 than 2006, so the proportion of the children in poverty who live in a workless family can increase even if the poverty risk among that group falls.

Note also that, among the group of children in poverty, there has been a compositional shift towards those with workless parents (particularly workless lone parents) since the last update to BBS. This becomes particularly relevant when modelling the costs of reducing child poverty to target (see Section 3.3), as children in households with workless parents tend to be further below the poverty line than those with working parents, and therefore more expensive to lift out of poverty.

3.3 Packages to meet the child poverty target for 2010

To meet the 2010 target, a policy package needs to reduce 2010 child poverty by around 600,000 relative to what child poverty would have been under the policy baseline.

The packages that will enable the 2010 target to be met are slightly different in the case where we account separately for non-reporting of benefits and tax credits in HBAI. This is for two reasons: first, the baseline forecasts are different when we adjust separately for non-reporting, which changes the number of children that need to be lifted out of poverty in order to hit the target; second, increasing benefits and tax credits has less effect on simulated incomes if we assume that some of these extra benefits and tax credits will not be reported as income in the 2010–11 FRS. We report results both with and without this separate adjustment in Table 8; Table A3.2 (in Appendix 3) also shows the results without our new poverty line adjustment (see Section 3.1), as this corresponds to the methodology used in BBS.

When not separately accounting for non-reporting in HBAI, the five policy packages that would reduce child poverty by about 600,000 under the central forecast are (all financial values are in 2010–11 prices which, given HM Treasury predictions about inflation, are little different from current prices, and all policies are on top of the 2010 policy baseline):

1. **Child Tax Credit** only option: Increase the child element of the Child Tax Credit by £650 per year (about £12.50 per week, or a rise of 29%).

2. **Child Benefit** only option: Increase Child Benefit by £12.50 per week for all children (a rise of 63% for the first child and 95% for subsequent children).

3. **Child Tax Credit plus large families (CB)**: Increase the child element of the Child Tax Credit by £475 per year (about £9.13 per week, or a 21% rise), and introduce a higher rate of Child Benefit for the third and subsequent children that is £20 per

week higher than that of the second child (or 152% higher than Child Benefit would otherwise be for the third and subsequent children).

4. **Child Tax Credit plus large families (CTC)**: Increase the child element of the Child Tax Credit by £490 per year (about £9.42 per week, or a 22% rise), and introduce additional payments for the third and subsequent children paid with the family element of the Child Tax Credit of £20 per week (a 4% increase in the family element for those with three children, or twice that increase for those with four children, etc.). The difference with the above is that the extra support for the third and subsequent children is tapered away from families with incomes over £50,000.

5. **Child Tax Credit plus WTC for couples:** Increase the child element of the Child Tax Credit by £330 per year (about £6.35 per week, or a 15% rise), and increase Working Tax Credit for couples with children by £2,100 per year (£40.38 per week, or a 56% rise).

When accounting separately for non-reporting in HBAI, the five policy packages that would reduce child poverty by about 600,000 under the central forecast if they were implemented on top of the baseline are (financial values in 2010–11 prices as before):

1. **Child Tax Credit** only option: Increase the child element of the Child Tax Credit by £725 per year (about £13.94 per week, or a rise of 32%).

2. **Child Benefit** only option: Increase child benefit by £13.95 per week for all children (a rise of 70% for the first child and 106% for subsequent children).

3. **Child Tax Credit plus large families (CB)**: Increase the child element of the Child Tax Credit by £550 per year (about £10.58 per week, or a 25% rise), and introduce a higher rate of Child Benefit for the third and subsequent children that is £20 per week higher than that of the second child (or 152% higher than Child Benefit would otherwise be for the third and subsequent children).

4. **Child Tax Credit plus large families (CTC)**: Increase the child element of the Child Tax Credit by £575 per year (about £11.06 per week, or a 26% rise), and introduce additional payments for the third and subsequent children paid with the family element of the Child Tax Credit of £20 per week (a 4% increase in the family element for those with three children, or twice that increase for those with four children, etc.). The difference with the above is that the extra support for the third and subsequent children is tapered away from families with incomes over £50,000.

5. **Child Tax Credit plus WTC for couples:** Increase the child element of the Child Tax Credit by £525 per year (about £10.10 per week, or a 23% rise), and increase Working Tax Credit for couples with children by £2,100 per year (£40.38 per week, or a 56% rise).

In all packages that increase Child Benefit or Child Tax Credit rates, the associated allowances in Housing Benefit and Council Tax Benefit are also increased.

These five policy packages bring child poverty in 2010 to a level broadly consistent with the government's target (which is about 1.7 million children, or a child poverty rate of 13.2%) but with differing costs. Table 8 shows poverty rates if these five packages were implemented, together with the cost relative to the central forecast under the policy baseline. It also shows the impact of these packages on the combined relative low income and material deprivation measure of poverty.

Table 8. Five packages that bring child poverty close to target in 2010 under the central forecast, with costs relative to the central forecast under the policy baseline

Policy	BHC child poverty rate		Material deprivation poverty rate		Cost (£ billion)		Cost per child taken out of poverty (£1,000s)	
	Adjustment for non-take-up	Adjustment for non-take-up and non-reporting	Adjustment for non-take-up	Adjustment for non-take-up and non-reporting	Adjustment for non-take-up	Adjustment for non-take-up and non-reporting	Adjustment for non-take-up	Adjustment for non-take-up and non-reporting
Memo: actual 2006–7 HBAI	22.3		15.6		n/a	n/a	n/a	n/a
Baseline (central forecast)	17.8	18.0	13.7–14.1	13.7–14.0	0	0	0	0
Child Tax Credit option	13.3	13.2	10.7–11.4	10.4–10.7	4.2	4.7	6.9	7.7
Child Benefit option	13.2	13.2	10.7–11.2	10.3–10.5	8.9	9.9	14.3	15.9
Child Tax Credit plus large families (CB)	13.1	13.2	10.3–10.8	9.6–9.9	4.7	5.2	7.5	8.4
Child Tax Credit plus large families (CTC)	13.3	13.2	10.2–10.8	9.6–9.9	4.3	4.9	7.1	7.9
Child Tax Credit plus higher WTC for couples	13.1	13.2	11.3–11.8	10.5–10.9	5.6	7.0	8.9	11.4
Memo: 2010–11 target	13.2		10.4		n/a	n/a	n/a	n/a

Notes: All costs are relative to the central forecast under the policy baseline and in 2010–11 prices, although forecast inflation between 2008–09 and 2010–11 is negligible. Box 4 explains why a range is given for the material deprivation and relative income measure.
Source: Authors' calculations based on FRS 2005–06 and 2006–07 using TAXBEN and various assumptions specified in the text.

Looking at the column headed 'Adjustment for non-take-up', the two policies that focus extra resources on larger families are forecast just to meet the 2010–11 target under the more optimistic of our two forecasts, but the package that is the cheapest at hitting the main relative low income target is forecast to fall just short of the 2010–11 combined relative low income and material deprivation target. For all packages, the more pessimistic of our forecasts of combined relative low income and material deprivation lie some way above the 2010–11 target, and this means that the government cannot merely rely on falls in the number of children below 70% of the median income in order to hit the combined relative low income and material deprivation target; there will also need to be falls in the proportion of children experiencing material deprivation. The column headed 'Adjustment for non-take-up and non-reporting' shows lower levels of combined relative low income and material deprivation under all packages, with almost all forecast to meet the government's target. It is not clear why the apparently small difference in the way that incomes are simulated has such a large impact on this measure of poverty, but it most likely reflects that the underlying relationship between material deprivation and disposable income varies depending on whether one calculates disposable income allowing only for non-take-up, or for non-take-up and non-reporting. Note that the fact that hypothetical policies are analysed in this paper does not mean that the authors are recommending that such policies be introduced.

Of the five policies looked at here, the cheapest is to increase the child element of the Child Tax Credit. This costs about £4.7 billion, or £7,700 per child taken out of poverty, when we adjust for non take-up and non-reporting. When we do not separately adjust for non-reporting, the projected cost is £4.2 billion, or £6,900 per child taken out of poverty.

All costs in Table 8 are the costs of hitting the target conditional on the central scenario occurring. The bad recession scenario would change the costs of hitting the target. However, we have modelled the costs conditional upon the bad recession scenario occurring, and they are very similar to the costs presented in Table 8. This is unsurprising, since we have already established that the bad recession scenario makes little difference to the 2010 level of child poverty under the policy baseline (although, as discussed (see Section 3.2), we would expect a bad recession significantly to reduce the government's tax revenues – while it does not seriously affect the *cost* of hitting the target, it does significantly affect the *affordability* of hitting the target).

Note that, since the child element of the Child Tax Credit is a means-tested benefit, increasing it will harm financial work incentives,[13] which we do not model. Child Benefit is a universal benefit, and so has no impact on the gain from working but, because it is not targeted at poorer families, the cost of this option is about twice that of relying on the means-tested child element of the Child Tax Credit. Any change in child-contingent support might also affect fertility assumptions (see Brewer, Ratcliffe and Smith, 2008, for example), which again we do not allow for here.

---

[13] Adam, Brewer and Shephard (2006) discuss and quantify the conflict between redistributing income to the poor and improving work incentives. For lone parents, increasing the child element of the Child Tax Credit reduces the financial gain from working for some high-wage individuals, and leaves it untouched for those on a lower wage. For those lone parents in work, increasing the child element of the Child Tax Credit may increase the effective marginal tax rate, or extend the range of income over which an individual faces a tax credit withdrawal, dulling incentives to increase earnings. The first earner in a couple is affected in the same way as a lone parent. The second earner in a couple, though, is much more likely to find that the financial gain from working at all is reduced by increasing the child element of the Child Tax Credit. See chapter 5 of Adam, Brewer and Shephard (2006) for a longer discussion; see also Brewer, Saez and Shephard (2009, forthcoming).

Figure 3a. Budget constraint for a lone parent with two children earning £6 per hour under the 2010 Child Tax Credit package

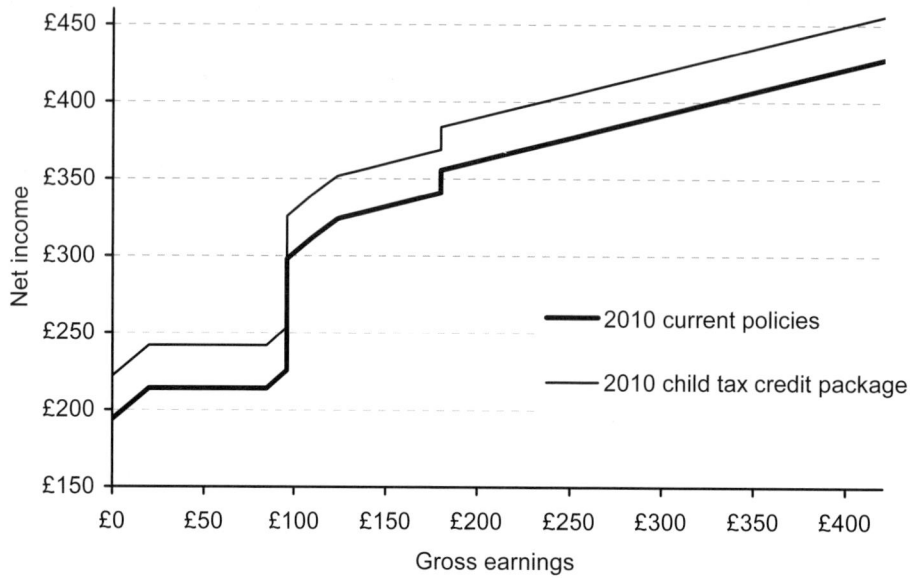

Note: 2010 prices. Assumed no housing costs, council tax liability or spending on child care or free school meals.

Figure 3b. Budget constraint for a second earner in a couple with two children earning £6 per hour, where the first earner earns £20,000 per year

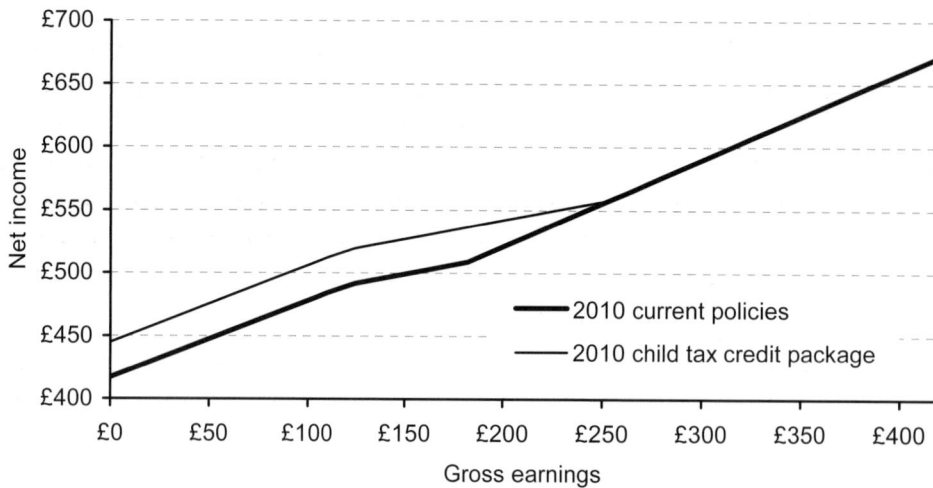

Note: 2010 prices. Assumed no housing costs, council tax liability or spending on child care or free school meals.

Figures 3a and 3b show the effect of the Child Tax Credit package on the budget constraints of two family types. We can see that, for a low-income lone parent, the package shifts the budget constraint up with no change in marginal effective tax rates; although, for a higher-income lone parent (not shown), the package increases the range over which they face a very high marginal effective tax rate. For the second earner in a couple, the package increases the marginal effective tax rate over a range of income.

Tables 9 and 10 show the child poverty rates among various subgroups and the composition of the group of children in poverty in 2010 if the most cost-efficient package (the increase in the Child Tax Credit) were implemented. In comparison to the baseline, this package particularly reduces the poverty risk among workless lone parents (who tend to be close to the poverty line), and therefore results in a small compositional shift among children in poverty towards those in couple families.

The most recent update to BBS (an assessment made after Budget 2008) suggested that hitting the 2010 target would cost about £2.8 billion (in 2008–09 prices). We have since introduced a poverty line adjustment in our simulated income distribution and added a second way of accounting for non-take-up of tax credits and benefits. For comparison with BBS and subsequent updates to it, we have included results without the poverty line adjustment in Appendix 3. Appendix 3 shows that if we were to follow the methodology of BBS – i.e. without adjusting the poverty line and without accounting separately for non-reporting – we would now be estimating a cost of £2.7 billion (in 2010–11 prices). The total costs of hitting the target have thus stayed similar, but the cost per child taken out of poverty is £6,200 when using the same method as BBS, which is about £1,000 more per child than we projected in our previous update.

An explanation for this is that the children in poverty in our simulated income distribution now tend to be further below the poverty line, and thus more expensive to lift out of poverty, due to lower employment. Many children who are estimated to fall below the poverty line will do so because their parents lose their jobs, and they will therefore tend to have very low incomes. Being a long way from the poverty line, children in these families will be particularly expensive to lift out of poverty. This can also be seen when comparing the simulated 2010 income distribution that we now project with the one underlying the last update to BBS, shown in Figures 4a and 4b. Note that when comparing the new results to the results obtained in BBS, it is useful to consider the new results without the poverty line adjustment, since this adjustment was not made in BBS. Therefore, we include the (lower) unadjusted poverty line in Figure 4b. For the same reason, the income distribution shown in Figure 4b is the one that we project when we do not adjust for non-reporting, as in BBS.

Figure 4a shows that, under our previous simulations, the poverty line in 2010–11 was projected to lie just above (i.e. to the right of) the modal point of the income distribution, meaning that a relatively large number of children could be moved out of poverty at relatively low cost. We can see from Figure 4b that this is not the case under our updated simulations: the densest part of the simulated income distribution for children in 2010 is now above the poverty line, and the distribution more than halves in density between the poverty line and £30 (per week) below the poverty line (note that the high density of the income distribution around the poverty line highlights the considerable uncertainty over forecasts of child poverty). Therefore, fewer children can now be brought out of poverty at low cost.

Table 9. Child poverty by family type/employment status in 2010 after implementing the most cost-efficient policy

	Lone parent		Couple		Workless lone parent		Part-time working lone parent		Full-time working lone parent		Workless couple		One full-time worker couple		Two full-time worker couple		One full-time one part-time couple		Zero full-time and one or two part-time couple		Self-employed couple	
	Number	%	Number	%	Number	%	Number	%	Number	%	Number	%	Number	%	Number	%	Number	%	Number	%	Number	%
2006–07 HBAI	1,156,983	36.5	1,710,430	17.7	929,770	57.5	181,745	19.4	45,584	7.4	436,973	68.1	471,802	20.2	39,116	2.4	91,167	3.2	304,995	46.6	363,361	23.4
2006–07 simulated	1,092,720	34.8	1,566,035	16.1	879,745	54.0	185,170	21.9	27,805	4.2	422,673	58.1	354,889	15.2	23,703	1.3	79,924	3.2	211,963	54.4	472,883	24.7
2010–11 predicted, take-up and non-reporting adjustment	624,730	19.2	1,069,483	11.2	520,151	29.8	93,456	10.9	21,123	3.0	323,645	42.4	212,786	8.7	18,180	1.0	50,624	2.1	126,294	32.3	337,954	18.1
2010–11 predicted, take-up adjustment	601,016	18.2	1,108,647	11.6	493,857	28.3	90,857	10.6	16,302	2.3	416,585	54.6	210,177	8.6	10,354	0.6	44,943	1.9	151,666	38.8	274,922	14.7

Table 10. Composition of child poverty count in 2010 after implementing the most cost-efficient policy

	Lone parent	Couple	Workless lone parent	Part-time working lone parent	Full-time working lone parent	Workless couple	One full-time worker couple	Two full-time worker couple	One full-time one part-time couple	Zero full-time and one or two part-time couple	Self-employed couple
2006–07 HBAI	40%	60%	32%	6%	2%	15%	16%	1%	3%	11%	13%
2006–07 simulated	41%	59%	33%	7%	1%	16%	13%	1%	3%	8%	18%
2010–11 predicted, take-up and non-reporting adjustment	37%	63%	30%	5%	1%	19%	12%	1%	3%	7%	20%
2010–11 predicted, take-up adjustment	35%	65%	29%	5%	1%	24%	12%	1%	3%	9%	16%

Figure 4a. Simulated income distribution for children in 2010–11 underlying the last update to BBS[14]

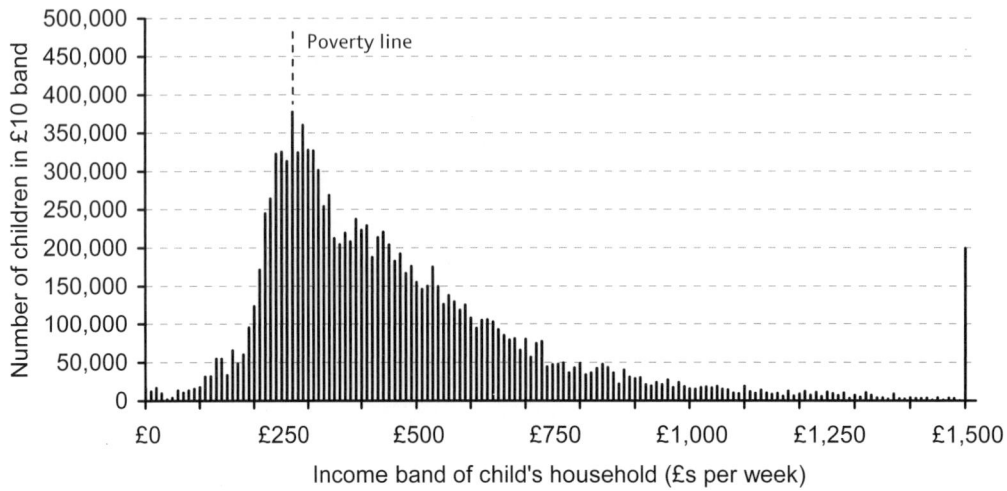

Sources: Authors' calculations using FRS 2005–06 and 2006–07, TAXBEN and assumptions specified in the text.

Figure 4b. New simulated income distribution for children in 2010–11

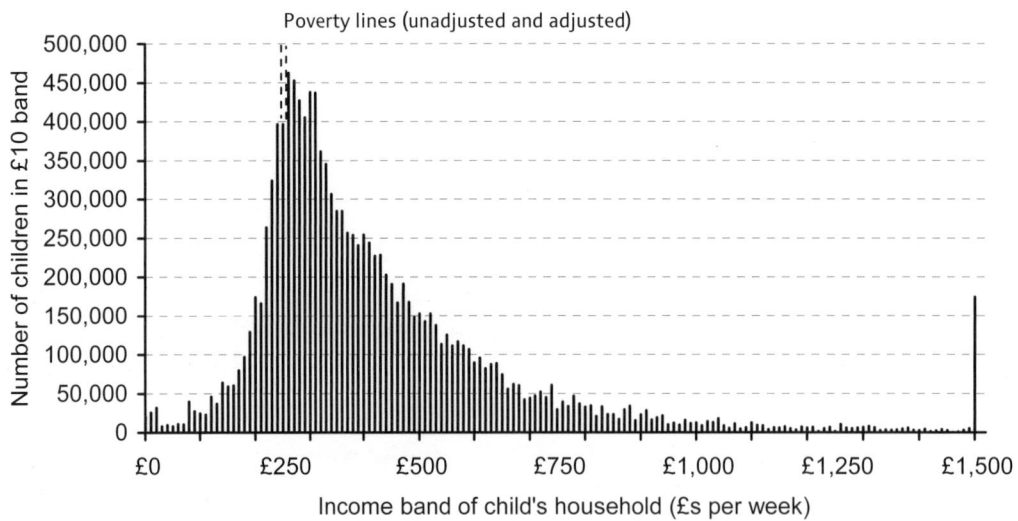

Source: Authors' calculations using FRS 2005–06 and 2006–07, TAXBEN and assumptions specified in the text.

---

[14] See Q67 of oral evidence in House of Commons Treasury Committee (2008).

4. Child poverty in 2020–21

This section presents our simulations for child poverty in 2020–21, and our estimates of what it might cost to hit the government's target. We continue to use the new poverty line adjustment, but results without this adjustment are given in Tables A3.3 and A3.4 (in Appendix 3). As explained in Section 2, we follow BBS in defining abolition of child poverty as having a rate equal to or below 5%, and we do not consider the combined relative income and material deprivation measure of child poverty.

4.1 Simulating the level of child poverty in 2020–21

Table 11 shows real annual median income growth between 2006 and 2020 and predicted levels of child poverty in 2020 under the policy baseline, for each of the three lone parent employment scenarios that we look at (see Box 5 for details). As with our 2010 projections, the policy baseline represents a 'no change' policy scenario, with 'usual' uprating rules followed except for where commitments have already been made to the contrary (see Table A2.2 in Appendix 2). However, one exception is that we assume that the per-child child element of the Child Tax Credit continues to be uprated in line with earnings (not prices) between 2010 and 2020, as is the current practice, but note that this has not yet been accounted for in the government's public finance projections after the end of the current parliament. If we instead assumed that the child element of the Child Tax Credit would be uprated in line with prices between 2010 and 2020, then, under the middle employment scenario, child poverty in 2020 would be about 500,000 (almost 4 percentage points) higher and the government would spend about £2.5 billion less in current prices.

Box 5. Lone parent employment scenarios for 2020

The child poverty rate is affected by the amount of paid work done by parents. Brewer et al. (2006, ch. 4) showed that the reduced number of children in workless families was a major contributor to the fall in child poverty between 1998 and 2004. The UK government has sought to increase the amount of paid work done by parents as one way of reducing child poverty, and may continue to do so.

Gregg, Harkness and MacMillan (2006) considered prospects for lone parents' employment rates in 2010 and 2020, both under then-existing policies (tax and benefit policies and labour market policies affecting lone parents) and under potential policy changes. As in BBS, we draw from this work to model three lone parent employment scenarios for 2020, shown below.

We assume no displacement in the labour market when lone parents find work (i.e. when lone parent employment increases, total employment increases by the same number).

Lone parents, % in work:
- Demographic changes only: 65.6%
- Demographic changes plus welfare-to-work policies: 70%
- Demographic changes, welfare-to-work and uprating Working Tax Credit in line with earnings: 73%

Source: Based on Gregg, Harkness and MacMillan (2006).

Table 11. Forecast child poverty in 2020–21 under the policy baseline

Lone parent employment assumption	Take-up adjustment	Before Housing Costs			After Housing Costs		
		Real annual growth in median income, 2006–20 (%)	Children in poverty (millions)	Child poverty rate (%)	Real annual growth in median income, 2006–20 (%)	Children in poverty (millions)	Child poverty rate (%)
Low	Take-up only	1.2	3.2	23.5	1.1	4.4	32.9
Low	Take-up and non-reporting	1.2	3.1	23.1	1.1	4.5	33.0
Middle	Take-up only	1.2	3.1	23.0	1.1	4.4	32.5
Middle	Take-up and non-reporting	1.2	3.1	22.7	1.1	4.4	32.5
High	Take-up only	1.2	3.1	22.7	1.1	4.3	32.2
High	Take-up and non-reporting	1.2	3.0	22.4	1.1	4.3	32.1

Source: Authors' calculations based on FRS 2005–06 and 2006–07 using TAXBEN and assumptions specified in the text.

Table 11 shows the following:

- The child poverty rate will be about 5 percentage points higher in 2020 than in 2010 under current policies. This reflects the fact that the current practice of uprating benefits in line with prices would result in benefits growing less quickly than median income between 2010 and 2020, causing additional households with children to fall below the poverty line.

- This rise in child poverty under the policy baseline between 2010 and 2020 more than offsets the reduction in child poverty that we project between 2006 and 2010 (which occurs largely as a result of measures announced by the government in Budgets 2007 and 2008), so that the child poverty rate in 2020 would be slightly higher than it was in 2006.

Tables 12 and 13 show the poverty risk by subgroup and the composition of the group in poverty in 2020, under the 2020 policy baseline and assuming the middle employment scenario. They show that the poverty risk for children in workless families is significantly larger than in 2010, but children in workless families will still account for a smaller proportion of the overall child poverty count than in 2020 because the employment rate in 2020 is higher than currently anticipated in 2010 (see Tables 4 and 5 for comparison).

Table 12. Child poverty by family type/employment status in 2020 under the policy baseline and middle lone parent employment scenario

	Lone parent		Couple		Workless lone parent		Part-time working lone parent		Full-time working lone parent		Workless couple		One full-time worker couple		Two full-time worker couple		One full-time one part-time couple		Zero full-time and one or two part-time couple		Self-employed couple	
	Number	%	Number	%	Number	%	Number	%	Number	%	Number	%	Number	%	Number	%	Number	%	Number	%	Number	%
2020–21 predicted, take-up and non-reporting adjustment	1,213,656	33.5	1,846,451	18,68	825,726	56.9	325,264	26.7	62,666	6.6	404,071	65.8	532,752	22.8	25,011	1.3	100,096	3.8	226,391	56.2	558,130	28.1
2020–21 predicted, take-up adjustment	1,205,790	33.3	1,902,210	19.3	817,875	56.4	330,909	27.2	57,006	6.0	463,867	75.5	550,510	23.6	21,652	1.2	105,246	3.9	229,408	57.0	531,527	26.7

Table 13. Composition of child poverty count in 2020 by family type/employment status under the policy baseline and middle lone parent employment scenario

	Lone parent	Couple	Workless lone parent	Part-time working lone parent	Full-time working lone parent	Workless couple	One full-time worker couple	Two full-time worker couple	One full-time one part-time couple	Zero full-time and one or two part-time couple	Self-employed couple
2020–21 predicted, take-up and non-reporting adjustment	40%	60%	27%	11%	2%	13%	17%	1%	3%	7%	18%
2020–21 predicted, take-up adjustment	39%	61%	26%	11%	2%	15%	18%	1%	3%	7%	17%

4.2 Packages to meet the child poverty target for 2020

We have modelled the effect of the following policies between 2010 and 2020, all assuming that the government adopts the most cost-efficient package to hit the 2010 child poverty target (increasing the child element of the Child Tax Credit):

1. **Selective earnings indexation**: Follow the current practices for uprating benefits and tax credits between 2010 and 2020, by uprating the per-child element of the Child Tax Credit in line with earnings and indexing all other benefits and tax credits to prices (the difference between this and the 2020 baseline is only that this assumes the implementation of the 2010 Child Tax Credit package).

2. **Comprehensive earnings indexation for parents**: Uprate all benefits and tax credits for parents in line with earnings,[15] and all benefits and tax credits for non-parents in line with prices.

3. **Over-indexation plus higher rate of Working Tax Credit for couples with children:** As 2. above, except for Income Support applicable amounts and the child element of the Child Tax Credit, which are uprated by 5.5% per year in real terms for parents; and introduce a higher rate of Working Tax Credit for couples with children that is 60% higher than the rate for lone parents.

In all packages that increase Child Benefit or Child Tax Credit rates, the associated allowances in Housing Benefit and Council Tax Benefit are also increased.

The generosity of the over-indexation package was determined such that, when combined with a halving of non-take-up of tax credits and benefits, child poverty in 2020 could be brought down to about 5% when adjusting for non-take-up only[16] (see the bottom of Table 14). A substantial reduction in non-take-up is plausible, given the generosity of the benefit and tax credit payments in the over-indexation package.

In Table 14 we show poverty rates for these packages under each of the three employment scenarios together with the cost in each case. All costs are relative to the low employment scenario under the baseline: for the higher employment scenarios, we give the costs net of the savings that arise from more lone parents being in work: this means that we are allowing the government to spend the extra tax revenue and the reduced spending on tax credits and means-tested benefits.

Financial values in this section are in current prices and, in brackets, in GDP-adjusted prices. The GDP adjustment is designed to take account of the fact that the costs of a package in 2020 may seem misleadingly large (even in current prices) because GDP is currently a lot smaller than we would expect it to be in 2020. The GDP-adjusted figures are therefore derived by calculating the proportion of 2020 GDP that the package will

---

[15] This includes Income Support, Housing Benefit applicable amounts, all of the Child and Working Tax Credits amounts and thresholds and Child Benefit. One exception was the threshold at which the family element of the Child Tax Credit was withdrawn, which was increased in line with prices: comprehensive earnings indexation would only increase the cost of this policy without helping families in poverty.

[16] In the scenario where the non-take-up rate is halved, we have not included projections using the non-take-up and non-reporting adjustment because, with that adjustment, the 'implied' take-up rate is different from the take-up rate as recorded by administrative data (because we do not count non-reported benefits and tax credits in the FRS as being 'taken up').

cost, and taking the same proportion of current GDP to get the GDP-adjusted cost (see Table A2.1 in Appendix 2 for our assumptions about inflation and nominal GDP). For example, we estimate that the selective earnings indexation package under the middle employment scenario would cost £3.9 billion in current prices. This is equivalent to spending £2.9 billion in current prices now, and subsequently indexing it to nominal GDP until 2020.

Table 14. Three packages to move towards the child poverty target in 2020, conditional on implementing the most cost-efficient package for 2010.

Policy	Lone parent employment	BHC poverty rate (%)		Cost (£ billion)	
		Adjust-ment for non-take-up	Adjust-ment for non-take-up and non-reporting	Adjust-ment for non-take-up	Adjust-ment for non-take-up and non-reporting
Baseline (without 2010 package)	Low	23.5	23.1	0.0 (0.0)	0.0 (0.0)
	Middle	23.0	22.7	−0.7 (−0.5)	−0.7 (−0.5)
	High	22.7	22.4	−1.1 (−0.8)	−1.1 (−0.8)
Selective earnings indexation	Low	17.4	16.5	4.6 (3.4)	5.1 (3.8)
	Middle	17.2	16.2	3.9 (2.9)	4.4 (3.2)
	High	17.0	16.0	3.4 (2.5)	4.0 (3.0)
Comprehensive earnings indexation for parents	Low	13.1	13.1	12.7 (9.4)	13.4 (9.9)
	Middle	12.9	12.8	12.2 (9.0)	12.7 (9.4)
	High	12.8	12.6	11.6 (8.6)	12.3 (9.1)
Over-indexation plus higher rate of Working Tax Credit for couples with children	Low	7.0	8.5	30.5 (22.5)	31.5 (23.3)
	Middle	6.9	8.4	29.8 (22.0)	30.8 (22.7)
	High	6.9	8.4	29.2 (21.6)	30.3 (22.4)
Over-indexation plus higher rate of Working Tax Credit for couples with children, with non-take-up of tax credits and benefits halved	Low	4.9	n/a	37.8 (28.0)	n/a
	Middle	4.8	n/a	37.1 (27.4)	n/a
	High	4.8	n/a	36.6 (27.0)	n/a

Note: Costs are in current prices and, in brackets, in GDP-adjusted prices.
Source: Authors' calculations based on FRS 2005–06 and 2006–07 using TAXBEN and assumptions specified in the text.

Selective earnings indexation, where everything but the child element of the Child Tax Credit is uprated in line with prices between 2010 and 2020, results in the child poverty rate climbing back almost to the 2010 baseline level: many of the children brought out of poverty by the 2010 package would fall below the poverty line again by 2020 as the income that those just above the poverty line would receive from benefits and tax credits would not keep pace with increases in median income.

Comprehensive earnings indexation for parents between 2010 and 2020 reduces the child poverty rate very slightly between 2010 and 2020 (conditional on implementing the 2010 package). Earnings indexation of benefits helps to equalise the rates at which incomes grow in different parts of the income distribution, which acts to keep relative poverty measures constant, but there are two reasons why the child poverty rate may fall under this package: first, we are allowing the lone parent employment rate to rise between 2010 and 2020; second, increasing benefits in line with average earnings usually implies a small rise in benefits relative to the poverty line (all other things remaining constant, fiscal drag means that median income will usually grow more slowly than average earnings).

If the preferred 2020 target were a child poverty rate of 5%, none of the uprating policies would be enough to meet the target without a reduction in non-take-up of benefits and tax credits. A package that over-indexes income support and the child element of the Child Tax Credit and introduces a higher rate of Working Tax Credit for couples with children brings child poverty closest to target, at a cost of between £29 billion and £32 billion. Adjusting for non-take-up only, this reduces child poverty to just below 7%; adjusting for non-take-up and non-reporting, it reduces child poverty to just below 8.5%.

Only if the over-indexation package were implemented alongside a halving of non-take-up of benefits and tax credits could it bring child poverty to below 5% in 2020 (when adjusting for non-take-up only). This would be at a cost of around £38 billion relative to the low lone parent employment scenario under the baseline. Conditional on having implemented the Child Tax Credit package to hit the 2010 target, the additional cost of meeting the 2020 target in this way would be more like £33 billion. Note, however, that this projection is for the non-take-up adjustment only, not for the separate non-reporting adjustment. Table 14 suggests that, when adjusting for non-reporting in HBAI as well as non-take-up, the 2020 child poverty rate when the over-indexation package is implemented is somewhat higher, so a halving of non-take-up may still not be enough for HBAI to reveal a child poverty rate of below 5%, unless non-reporting of benefit and tax credit receipt in the FRS is reduced.

5. Sensitivities

In this section, we investigate the impact of alternative assumptions about lone parent employment in 2010 and differential earnings growth between 2010 and 2020. We find that the results are altered in the way we would expect, but are not overly sensitive to the changes.

To test the sensitivity of our results to the lone parent employment rate, we conducted a crude adjustment to the composition of lone parents. We decreased the number of workless lone parents and increased the number of working lone parents by the same amount in order to get a lone parent employment rate of 60% or 65%. The lone parents whom we 'moved into work' were split between part-time and full-time work based on the existing proportions of part-time lone parent workers relative to full-time lone parent workers, and it was assumed that the poverty risk within each group (workless lone parents, part-time working lone parents and full-time working lone parents) remained the same. This may be a 'generous' assumption for the child poverty rate, because we might expect lone parents who were previously workless to be more likely to do part-time work rather than full-time work than the group of lone parents who were already in work.

As we would expect, higher lone parent employment rates reduce the child poverty rate. The differences are not large, though. A 60% lone parent employment rate would reduce the child poverty rate by 0.4 percentage points, and a 65% lone parent employment rate would reduce the child poverty rate by a further 0.5 percentage points (see Table 15). Given that lone parent employment has recently been broadly flat, that we are entering a recession and that we are forecasting only two years ahead, the chances of child poverty being brought significantly below our central forecast by rising lone parent employment look small.

Table 15. Results of 2010 lone parent employment sensitivity test

Scenario	Child poverty rate under the 2010 baseline (%)	
	Adjustment for non-take-up	Adjustment for non-take-up and non-reporting
Central	17.8	18.0
Lone parent employment of 60%	17.4	17.6
Lone parent employment of 65%	16.9	17.1

Source: Authors' calculations based on FRS 2005–06 and 2006–07 using TAXBEN and assumptions specified in the text.

In recent years, real earnings have not grown uniformly across the earnings distribution (i.e. if recent trends were to continue, the rate at which we would expect someone's earnings to grow would depend on how much they already earn). We assumed uniform annual real earnings growth between 2010 and 2020 of 2%. In this sensitivity test, we maintain this average real earnings growth rate but allow different deciles in the earnings distribution to have an earnings growth rate that differs from the growth rate of average earnings. These decile-specific divergences from the average earnings growth rate are derived from the pattern of differential earnings growth between 2001 and 2006, using the Retail Price Index (RPI) and FRS data on nominal earnings over the period. Table 16 gives our assumed average annual real earnings growth between 2010 and 2020 for each decile in the earnings distribution. Table 17 reports the results of the sensitivity test (we assumed the middle lone parent employment scenario).

The effect of differential earnings growth is to reduce child poverty, which is not surprising given that we have extrapolated from differential earnings growth in the period 2001–06, when the bottom decile experienced the strongest growth (see Table 16). The effect is very small indeed, however, at about one-tenth of a percentage point.

Table 16. Average annual real earnings growth rates assumed for the differential earnings growth sensitivity test, by decile

| | Decile of the earnings distribution | | | | | | | | | |
	1	2	3	4	5	6	7	8	9	10
Assumed average annual real earnings growth rate between 2010 and 2020 (%)	4.3	2.6	2.1	1.7	1.5	1.6	1.7	2.1	2.4	1.9

Source: Authors' calculations using FRS 2001–02 to 2006–07 data on nominal earnings, deflated by the RPI.

Table 17. Results of differential earnings growth sensitivity test for 2020 (assuming the middle lone parent employment scenario)

Earnings growth scenario	Child poverty rate under the 2020 baseline (%)	
	Adjustment for non-take-up	Adjustment for non-take-up and non-reporting
Uniform earnings growth	23.0	22.7
Differential earnings growth	22.9	22.6

Source: Authors' calculations based on figures shown in Table 16 and FRS 2005–06 and 2006–07, using TAXBEN and assumptions specified in the text.

6. Conclusions

The current UK government has an explicit target for child poverty in 2010, and a goal for 2020 that has not yet been precisely quantified. The aim of this paper has been to update our previous forecast of the prospects for child poverty in 2010 and 2020 under current government policies, and to illustrate the impact of various tax and benefit policies that could be implemented in 2010 and 2020.

Our analysis suggests that, under present tax and benefit policies, there will be 2.3 million children in poverty in 2010. This would be a reduction in the child poverty count of about 600,000 between 2006 and 2010, and would represent the lowest child poverty rate (as it is currently defined by the government) since 1985.[17] However, the reduction in child poverty actually required between 2006 and 2010 in order to hit the target is approximately twice as large as this, and our analysis has already taken account of policy changes that have been announced since 2006–07.

The current macroeconomic outlook is characterised by exceptional uncertainty. Our baseline scenario assumed a rise in unemployment from long-run levels and no growth in real earnings between 2007 and 2010. As a variant, we therefore also modelled the impact of a recession that is worse than currently expected (by HM Treasury) on the child poverty rate in 2010, through effects on employment and real earnings, although we acknowledge that we have approximated the impact of a recession in a very crude way (effectively assuming that all workers are equally likely to be made redundant). We found that the impact of a worse recession on child poverty is very small but acts to reduce relative child poverty, because lower real earnings and lower employment reduce median income (and thereby the poverty line), and this effect dominates the direct effect on low-income households with children. Our finding that a worse recession will reduce income inequality and relative poverty matches the historical experience in the UK. However, our projection is that a worse recession would increase poverty on the combined material deprivation and relative income measure, reflecting our view that material deprivation depends on absolute income, not relative income.

Of the five hypothetical policy packages that would bring child poverty to target in 2010, the most cost-efficient is to increase the child element of the Child Tax Credit by about 30% (compared to what the child element of the Child Tax Credit would otherwise have been in 2010). The precise package required to meet the target depends upon whether or not we adjust for non-reporting of benefit and tax credit receipt in the Family Resources Survey (which underpins the official HBAI measure of child poverty). If we do account for the fact that the FRS seems to under-record benefit and tax credit receipt, then the cost of meeting the target (according to the survey with which it is officially measured) is higher. The Child Tax Credit package that brings 2010 child poverty to target costs £4.7 billion if we take account of this non-reporting, and £4.2 billion if we do not (in 2010 prices, which are very similar to current prices). This would be an exceptionally large one-year package by historic standards.

This Child Tax Credit package would increase, on average, the marginal effective tax rates faced by working parents. In addition, the incentive to work at all would be dulled for the second worker in a couple, and these feedback effects – which would increase child

---

[17] Note that data on child poverty rates before 2000–01 are for Great Britain, not the UK.

poverty or increase the cost to government of meeting its targets – have not been reflected in the modelling. Policies that relied on universal benefits rather than means-tested ones would not affect marginal effective tax rates but could cost about twice as much.

If the government maintained its usual uprating rules after 2010, then, by 2020, the child poverty rate would be higher than it was in 2006, as the reductions that took place between 2006 and 2010 would be more than offset by the fact that tax credits and benefits (apart from the child element of the Child Tax Credit) grew less quickly than median income between 2010 and 2020. This would leave child poverty a very long way from being abolished, on any plausible definition of abolition. Similarly, if the 2010 Child Tax Credit package were introduced, but benefits and tax credits subsequently uprated in the same way as usual, the rise in child poverty by 2020 would undo almost all of the fall brought about by the 2010 package. If the child element of the Child Tax Credit were not uprated with earnings (at present, earnings uprating of the child element of the Child Tax Credit is not reflected in the government's public finance projections between 2010 and 2020), child poverty in 2020 would be higher still.

Of all the hypothetical tax and benefit policies that we looked at for the period 2010–20, only a large over-indexation package could reduce the child poverty rate to 5% by 2020, and only by assuming that non-take-up of tax credits and benefits is halved. This package involves uprating Income Support payments for parents and the per-child element of the Child Tax Credit by 5.5% per year in real terms between 2010 and 2020; uprating all other benefits and tax credits for parents in line with earnings; raising the Working Tax Credit by 60% for couples with children after it has been earnings-uprated between 2010 and 2020; and uprating benefits and tax credits for non-parents in line with prices between 2010 and 2020. This would cost about £37 billion in current prices (the cost could be even higher if we take account of the non-reporting of benefit and tax credit receipt in the FRS). But this package would substantially increase the number of parents facing high marginal effective tax rates, and it would mean that government support for families with children would be far higher than for those without, and both of these could mean that it is politically and economically unsustainable.

As before, this exercise is constrained by what it is possible to model: that is, where a particular policy has a reasonably predictable effect on household incomes. Some policies – such as improving the education levels of tomorrow's parents (see Machin and McNally, 2006; Blanden, Hansen and Machin, 2008) – will be fundamental to the long-term reduction in child poverty, but their results cannot readily be projected using these methods.

Furthermore, the uncertainties that surround any economic forecast are particularly prominent here, and more prominent than in our previous forecast due to the present macroeconomic outlook. The extent to which total employment, real earnings and parents' employment are affected by macro events, and the relative incidence of these effects on particular groups of people (i.e. low-income families with children relative to the median family), all have a bearing on child poverty rates.

The static nature of our simulation model is also important to note. The model gives us snapshots of the income distribution at a point in time, but does not track movements in and out of poverty. Again, this may be particularly important in this update due to the possibility that the macro economy will be volatile in the near term (so movements in and out of poverty may be relatively frequent).

Appendix 1. Methodology

This describes how future levels of child poverty in the UK were forecast using a micro-simulation model (TAXBEN). The procedure is largely the same as in Brewer, Browne and Sutherland (2006).

A1.1 Data

We use data on households in the UK from the Family Resources Survey for 2005–06 and 2006–07 combined. After dropping those households that we cannot use (because they are missing crucial information), we are left with 63,344 families, 16,518 of whom have dependent children. We amend the base data in two ways in order to construct an estimate of the population's characteristics in 2010 and 2020 (we call these the 'synthetic populations'):

- Changes in financial characteristics of households (such as levels of private (pre-transfer) incomes) are made by uprating variables in the data, using our projections of various price and earnings indices (see Section A1.2).

- Changes in other characteristics of households (e.g. household size, the number of lone parent or couple families and employment rates) are adjusted using re-weighting techniques. In other words, we do not adjust the values of these characteristics in our base data, but we do adjust the grossing weights that are applied to the base data to produce the synthetic populations (see Section A1.3).

A1.2 Uprating financial variables

In order to take into account changes that are likely to occur between the period covered by our base data and 2010 and 2020, we need to uprate the financial variables (mostly information about households' income). We use the actual Average Earnings Index (AEI) and the Retail Price Index from 2006 to the present, and Treasury forecasts (given in Table A2.1 in Appendix 2) thereafter wherever possible.

We chose to peg most financial variables to a forecast of nominal earnings growth, which we constructed from the Treasury's forecast of inflation (RPI) and our assumptions about real earnings growth.

Specifically, we assume that:

- Earnings from employment and self-employment, and incomes from private pensions, grow by 0% in real terms between 2007 and 2010 and 2% per year in real terms between 2010 and 2020. In our 'bad recession' scenario for 2010, real earnings were assumed to fall by 1% between 2007 and 2010. We also included a 'differential real earnings growth' scenario for 2020, where average real earnings grow by 2% per year but real earnings grow differently in different parts of the earnings distribution.

- Rents, water and sewerage rates and other deductions from income (see A1.5) are forecast to increase in line with nominal earnings.

- Minor components of income (see Table A2.2 in Appendix 2 for definitions) are uprated in line with inflation (RPI).

- We assume that the base rate will be 2% in 2010, which was its level when we obtained our results for this project, and 4.75% in 2020. This is used to calculate the amount of income that investments will yield.

- The total stock of savings and investments held by households is uprated in line with nominal GDP in TAXBEN (we have used the Treasury's forecasts for nominal GDP from the 2008 Pre-Budget Report, which take us up to 2013, and we assumed the same rate of nominal GDP growth between 2013 and 2020 as the Treasury forecasts between 2012 and 2013).

We then uprate the tax and benefit system using current uprating procedures, using the Treasury's forecasts for RPI and ROSSI, which are the price indices currently used to uprate taxes and benefits (subject to the proviso in the 2008 Pre-Budget Report that allowances, benefits and tax credits will not be cut in cash terms in April 2010 should RPI or ROSSI be negative). Table A2.2 in Appendix 2 gives full details.

A1.3 Re-weighting to reflect socio-demographic changes

The FRS data that are used are weighted to adjust for differential non-response to the survey, and they are calculated so that when added up over the whole sample, the number of people or households with certain characteristics matches a set of control totals (see Department for Work and Pensions, 2005).

We use re-weighting techniques to project the characteristics of the household population in 2010 and 2020. For example, if we expect the total number of households with characteristic x to rise between 2006 and 2010, then we re-weight the simulated 2010 population so that households with characteristic x are given more weight than they were in the base data. We use population projections for the UK in 2010 and 2020 by John Parsons and Phil Rees at the University of Leeds (Parsons and Rees, 2008) as the basis for the control totals for our 'synthetic populations' in 2010 and 2020.

The dimensions controlled for simultaneously in this way in our baseline forecasts included age group, household size, number of lone parents, number of couple parent families, region of residence, employment, housing tenure and ethnicity. We also used re-weighting to capture the impact of a particularly bad recession on employment in our 'bad recession' scenario for 2010, and to model the effects of different lone parent employment rates on child poverty in 2020 in our three lone parent employment scenarios. We did this by adjusting the relevant employment control totals that were used to derive the weights.

The set of control totals that we chose to use (see Table A2.3 in Appendix 2) was slightly different from the set we used in the last project. We wanted to harmonise what we control for as closely as possible with the official weights applied to the FRS data by DWP. We found that changing which dimensions are controlled for had a surprisingly large impact on poverty rates, and we could not perfectly mimic the set of control totals used by DWP (since we do not have credible forecasts for all such control totals). To the extent that our different set of control totals causes our simulated income distribution to differ from the HBAI-measured income distribution, our newly introduced poverty line adjustment should harmonise our simulation technique with HBAI measurement. The implicit assumption here is that a different set of control totals does not cause simulated changes in poverty to be different, though it may affect the simulated level of poverty at a point in time (see Section 3.1 for details of the poverty line adjustment).

The control total used for total employment in 2010 is not the control total provided in the demographic projections by Parsons and Rees. This is because this total was based on a long-run view of the economy's employment potential from the perspective of early 2006, but the short-term macroeconomic outlook suggests that such long-run considerations are an inappropriate guide to employment levels in 2010. We therefore apply a deduction to the employment total obtained from Parsons and Rees. This employment deduction was derived by looking at how the claimant count forecasts by HM Treasury have changed since the effects of the recession are likely to have been taken into account. We first use the claimant count assumption for end-2009 given in the 2007 Pre-Budget Report (HM Treasury, 2007a) as an approximation for the claimant count consistent with 'long-run' employment levels. We chose to do this on the basis that no deterioration in macroeconomic prospects of the scale currently expected was anticipated in November 2007. That claimant count assumption was 920,000. We then took the claimant count assumption for end-2010 from the 2008 Pre-Budget Report (HM Treasury, 2008) – the latest available – which was 1,550,000, and used the percentage difference between those two assumptions (68%) as an estimate of how much the recession will increase the claimant count from its long-run level. We then took the March 2008 International Labour Organisation (ILO) unemployment count to be an approximation for the unemployment level consistent with long-run employment levels, and assumed that the recession will increase it by the same proportion as the claimant count. We therefore deducted 68% of the March 2008 unemployment level from our 2010 employment total (this implicitly assumes no change in inactivity). Our new employment total gives an employment rate of about 72.5% in 2010. For the bad recession scenario for 2010, we deducted twice as much from our original employment total, giving an employment rate of about 69.5% in 2010.

The weights were calculated using CALMAR in the same way as in Brewer, Browne and Sutherland (2006), and are subject to the same limitations as were outlined in that report, quoted below:

> The re-weighting method simply controls for characteristics in a few dimensions, leaving joint distributions uncontrolled (e.g. typically we can get the number of lone parents and the number of children in each age group to match control totals, but the ages of children in lone parent families are not directly controlled for). Other relevant dimensions on which we have inadequate information for predictions are entirely uncontrolled (e.g. receipt of child support or hours of work). Furthermore, with a given sample size the number of dimensions that can be controlled for at once is limited. If the number of constraints becomes large it can become impossible to satisfy them, or some households have extremely high weights, making the policy simulation results unstable.

> Finally, the greater the difference between the world represented by the FRS data and the world that the re-weighting using projected control totals attempts to sketch out, the more difficult it is to find weights that

satisfy many controls simultaneously. Thus it was more difficult to calculate weights for 2020 than for 2010 and the distribution of weights in the 2020 scenarios is much wider than for 2010. The 2020 weighted results should therefore be treated with extra caution (pp. 54–55).

A1.4 Reflecting non-take-up and misreporting of benefits and tax credits

TAXBEN calculates what benefits and tax credits individuals and households are entitled to under hypothetical tax and benefit systems. However, not everyone who is entitled to benefits or tax credits will necessarily claim them. Some households may be unaware of their entitlement, or find it too time-consuming to claim, or find claiming means-tested benefits stigmatising, or dislike the uncertainty around overpayments or underpayments that surrounds tax credit receipt.

Assuming full take-up may mean that the micro-simulation model underestimates the level of child poverty, since it is generally the poor (rather than the median household) who are eligible to benefits and tax credits, and so it is the poor who will lose out if not all tax credits and benefits are claimed. Such an assumption will also mean that TAXBEN overestimates the cost to the government of increasing means-tested benefits and tax credits.

On the other hand, estimates from the FRS of the number of people receiving means-tested benefits and tax credits, and of the total amount spent on such programmes, tend to be lower than those based on administrative data, even when allowance is made for the less-than-full coverage of the FRS (i.e. it omits people not in private households). This suggests that there is misreporting of means-tested benefits and tax credit income in the FRS (specifically, under-reporting). Using take-up rates implied by the FRS may therefore underestimate the cost to the government of increasing means-tested benefits and tax credits, and it might also mean that TAXBEN overestimates the level of poverty (although it might mean the reverse if it is particularly households around the median that do not report income from tax credits).

It is not clear why the FRS underestimates the number of recipients of means-tested benefits or tax credits. It could be because recipients of means-tested benefits or tax credits are less likely to participate in the survey, and that the grossing weights fail to compensate for this form of differential non-response. On the other hand, it could be because recipients of means-tested benefits or tax credits are participating in the survey but the survey is not recording the fact that they receive means-tested benefits or tax credits.

We use official administrative data on the take-up rates of different benefits and tax credits, disaggregated by various subgroups. The latest take-up data for benefits come from the Department for Work and Pensions and are for 2006 (see Department for Work and Pensions, 2008b); the latest take-up data for tax credits come from HM Revenue & Customs and are for 2005 (see HM Revenue & Customs, 2008). Tables A2.4 and A2.5 in Appendix 2 have details of the take-up rates used (we used the midpoints of the upper and lower bounds for benefit take-up and the central estimate of tax credit take-up).

When simulating levels of child poverty, we use caseload take-up rates. These give the number of people claiming at least some of their entitlement to a benefit or tax credit as a percentage of all those who are entitled to it.

In the previous forecast, we adjusted for non-take-up by randomising take-up for all those eligible, with the probability of take-up being equal to the take-up rate from the administrative data for that benefit or tax credit for someone in the relevant subgroup. For this project, we have introduced a second way of accounting for non-take-up to mirror more closely take-up as recorded by the FRS (which we believe suffers from non-reporting of some tax credit and benefit receipt, and thus underestimates the true level of take-up). If someone is eligible but not reported as taking up a benefit in our base data from the FRS, then we assume that they will still not report taking up the benefit or tax credit in 2010 or 2020. For those who were not eligible in the base data (i.e. in 2005 or 2006) but become eligible by 2010 or 2020, we implement the randomisation that was used in BBS (described above). The motivation for this is that, because the take-up rates used to randomise are from administrative data (not the FRS), replacing some of the randomisation with a non-random procedure based on the FRS base data should bring us closer to forecasting child poverty as it is officially measured (i.e. using the FRS), which is the aim of the project.

Note that, in this paper (with the exception of some supplementary results in Appendix 3), all results are calculated using our new poverty line adjustment, which is designed to harmonise our simulated 2006 poverty rates with HBAI-measured 2006 poverty rates in order to account for any factors that make our simulation technique measure child poverty differently from HBAI. This means that, to the extent that non-reporting contributed to HBAI's relative 'pessimism' about child poverty rates in 2006, non-reporting is accounted for by the poverty line adjustment (regardless of the take-up procedure we use).

However, non-reporting will increase measured poverty by more when there are more tax credits and benefits to be reported (or not reported). Therefore, our simulated poverty rates using the old take-up procedure will tend to be lower than those using our new take-up procedure if tax credits and benefits are higher than they were in 2006. The differences between the numbers produced by the two procedures for our 2010 baseline should be relatively small, but we would expect the differences to be larger when analysing hypothetical policy packages that are designed to hit the 2010 target, as these involve very substantial increases in tax credits/benefits compared to 2006 levels. Because the new take-up procedure imposes lower implied take-up rates than the old one, it will generally be necessary to increase tax credits and benefits by more in order to reduce child poverty by a given amount (since less of the people around the poverty line will take up benefits and tax credits, more people who are relatively far below the poverty line will have to be brought above it in order to hit the target, and this will increase the cost). Tables A2.6 and A2.7 (in Appendix 2) show the implied take-up rates produced by the new take-up procedure under the 2010 policy baseline.

Note that if levels of misreporting in the FRS get better/worse between our base years (2005 and 2006) and 2010 or 2020, this will tend to lead us to over/underestimate the level of child poverty as measured by the FRS in 2010 or 2020. The assumption implicit in our forecasts using the new take-up procedure is therefore that the accuracy with which the FRS records benefit and tax credit receipt remains constant. The fact that the projected costs of hitting the target are higher when we use the new take-up procedure reflects the fact that it is more expensive to reduce HBAI-measured child poverty to target than to reduce 'actual' child poverty to target, since a given increase in tax credits or benefits has a smaller effect on HBAI-measured child poverty than on actual child poverty (although the fact that we make different adjustments to the poverty line for each take-up procedure may obscure this pattern).

We do not take account of the fact that it tends to be those households with small entitlements – households which are generally not the poorest in society – that are less likely to claim tax credits or means-tested benefits. This is another reason for reducing the element of randomisation in our adjustment for non-take-up and replacing it with a non-random procedure based on observed non-take-up in the past, but the element of randomisation that remains may still lead to an overestimate of the true level of child poverty. However, by splitting the population up into different groups which have rather different entitlements on average, we partially account for this.[18] We ignored any interactions between means-tested benefits and tax credits.

When estimating the costs of hypothetical policy packages, we use a random procedure based on expenditure take-up rates. In other words, if someone is entitled to a benefit or tax credit, we give them a probability of claiming (all of) it equal to the expenditure take-up rate for that benefit/tax credit for people in the same family type/tax credit unit. These take-up rates give the amount the government spends on benefits and tax credits as a percentage of what it would spend if everyone who was entitled claimed all of their entitlement, and are therefore the appropriate measure of take-up to use when costing a policy.

A1.5 Creating the HBAI definition of income, and calculating poverty rates

Given micro-simulated data on private incomes, liability to taxes and receipt of benefits and tax credits, we need to create a measure of disposable income that is as close as possible to that used in HBAI when calculating child poverty rates (the precise definition is given in Department for Work and Pensions, 2008a). To construct something broadly equivalent to this, we add together various sources of private (i.e. pre-transfer) income, subtract estimated tax liabilities, add estimated receipt of benefits and then subtract various 'deductions' from income. Table A2.8 gives full details of the various components of incomes.

Data on the deductions are derived partly from outputs from TAXBEN (e.g. Council Tax and contributions to a private pension), and partly taken from the official HBAI data set (because this is based on the FRS, we are able to merge the official HBAI data set with the data set produced by TAXBEN). We assume that this latter set of deductions (housing costs, child support paid for non-resident children and financial support given by parents to children who are students living away from home) increases over time in line with average earnings growth.

---

[18] For Income Support, Housing Benefit and Council Tax Benefit, the groups are: couples with children, lone parents, pensioners and working-age people without children. For tax credits, the groups are: those ineligible for tax credits, working-age people without children eligible for Working Tax Credit, workless families with children, working families with children eligible for Working Tax Credit and Child Tax Credit, working families with children entitled to no Working Tax Credit but more than just the family element of Child Tax Credit and those entitled to only the family element or less.

We can then create a measure of household equivalised income (by summing this final measure of disposable income across all members of a household, and dividing by various weights corresponding to different equivalence scales). The UK government has said that progress towards its 2010 and 2020 targets will be assessed using a measure of equivalised Before Housing Costs income based on the Modified OECD scale. We also report results using the same equivalence scales for After Housing Costs income.

We use these simulated data on the distribution of household disposable income to forecast median income, and thereby the poverty line.

A1.6 Forecasting material deprivation

Section 2 said that the government is now tracking three indicators of child poverty, one of which defines a child as poor if they live in a household with less than 70% of the median income and are materially deprived (see HM Treasury, 2007b; also Brewer et al., 2008, ch. 5).

We have provided forecasts of this measure in 2010–11, but not in 2020–21 (because the behaviour of these sorts of measures over a 14-year period is unknown). We have provided two forecasts:

- The first assumes that the material deprivation score of each family in our simulated 2010–11 data is the same as it was when the family appeared in the FRS in 2005–06 or 2006–07. This is not allowing any changes in incomes between 2005–06 or 2006–07 and 2010–11 to affect the material deprivation score, so the combined low income/material deprivation poverty rate will change only if the proportion of children with incomes below 70% of the median changes.

- The second uses multivariate regression techniques to predict the material deprivation score for each family given their simulated income in 2010–11. This was done by estimating a Tobit regression of the material deprivation score (ranging from 0 to 100, with a large fraction having a score of zero) on a number of household characteristics, and a 5th order polynomial in log of the simulated disposable income in 2006–07 interacted with the work status of the family (families were split into three groups according to whether: all adults were workless; any adults were self-employed; other). Details of the other characteristics in the regression and the coefficients are available on request from the authors. The coefficients from this regression were then used to predict the material deprivation score of each family in 2010–11, given simulated incomes in 2010–11. The predicted material deprivation score for each family included the residual for that family from the original Tobit regression on material deprivation in 2006–07. This achieves two things: it ensures that the simulated level of material deprivation in 2006–07 is equal to the actual level, and it ensures that the variance of predicted material deprivation in 2010–11 is similar to what it was in 2006–07 (if the residual had not been added to the predicted material deprivation score, then the distribution of predicted material deprivation scores in 2010–11 would have been much more compressed, and far fewer families would have a predicted score in excess of 25).

The first forecast can be thought of as a worst-case scenario (provided incomes are rising), because it does not allow any rise in income to lower material deprivation. The second forecast, though, should not be thought of as a best-case scenario. Berthoud,

Bryan and Bardasi (2004) showed that the relationship between changes in income and changes in material deprivation for individual households is much weaker than that between material deprivation and income when comparing different households, and the second forecast has used an estimate of the latter to predict the former. On the other hand, that study also showed that there was an unexplainable decline in material deprivation over time that could not be accounted for by rising incomes. The first of these points would suggest that we have overstated the decline in material deprivation between 2006–07 and 2010–11 (provided incomes rise), but the second would mean that we have understated the decline.

Appendix 2. Tables of our assumptions / procedures

Table A2.1. Assumptions about RPI, ROSSI, real earnings and nominal GDP growth for our baseline forecasts

Variable	2008–09	2009–10	2010–11	2011–12	2012–13	2013–14	2014–15 to 2020–21 (annual)
RPI inflation	5%	−2.25%	2.5%	4%	3.5%	3%	2.75%
ROSSI inflation	6.25%	0%	1.75%	2.5%	2.5%	2.5%	2.5%
Real earnings growth	0%	0%	0%	2%	2%	2%	2%
Nominal GDP growth	2.96%	1.16%	4.7%	5.7%	5.9%	5.8%	5.8%

Notes: All figures except for real earnings growth and 2014–15 to 2020–21 are from 'Table B1: Economic assumptions for the public finance projections' in HM Treasury (2008). Other figures are our own assumptions. Strictly speaking, we assume 0% real earnings growth over the whole period from 2008–09 to 2010–11, rather than the more restrictive assumption of 0% in each of the three years.

Table A2.2. Uprating rules used for baseline scenarios

Rule	What it's used to uprate
In line with prices	War Pensions Scholarship Income Income from government training schemes Other unearned income Allowances paid other than from spouse
In line with nominal earnings	Gross rent Water and sewerage rates Private pensions income Employment income Self-employment income Maintenance payments Allowances from absent spouse
In line with nominal GDP	Imputed capital from savings, annuities, property, stocks and shares and bonds
In line with RPI to previous September, rounded to nearest 5p	Child Benefit Severely disabled additional payments on Income Support and Housing Benefit Incapacity Benefit Carer's allowance Disability Living Allowance Attendance Allowance Severe Disablement Allowance Basic State Pension
In line with RPI to previous September, rounded to nearest £5	All Working Tax Credit amounts Disabled and Severely Disabled elements of the Child Tax Credit National Insurance Upper Earnings Limit
In line with RPI to previous September, increase rounded up to nearest £10	Income Tax personal allowances Income Tax married couples' allowances
In line with RPI to previous September, increase rounded up to nearest £100	Income Tax bands Threshold for withdrawal of older person's Income Tax allowances
In line with ROSSI to previous September, rounded to nearest 5p	Most Income Support rates Most Housing Benefit applicable amounts Non-dependent deductions for Income Support, Housing Benefit and Second Adult Council Tax Rebate
In line with ROSSI to previous September, rounded to nearest £1	Thresholds for non-dependent deductions for Income Support, Housing Benefit and Second Adult Council Tax Rebate
In line with Average Earnings Index to previous September, rounded to nearest 5p	Pension Credit guarantee amounts
In line with Average Earnings Index to previous September, rounded to nearest £5	Per-child element of the Child Tax Credit
Frozen	Winter Fuel Payments to pensioners Income Support and Housing Benefit disregards Family element of the Child Tax Credit Tax Credit thresholds

Note: Parameters in the tax and benefit system that are calculated as a function of other parameters continue to be calculated in the same manner.

Table A2.3. Control totals used to derive sets of weights for synthetic populations

Dimension	Categories
Population	n/a
Number of households	Scotland, London, all of UK
Household size	1 person
Region of residence	12 standard regions of GB
Age of individual	0–9, 10–15, 16–19 (dependent child), 16–19 (non-dependent), 20–24, 24–29, 30–44, 45–59, 60+
Number employed	n/a
Ethnicity (GB adults only)	Asian (GB only)
Lone parent families	n/a
Two-parent families by country of residence	n/a
Housing tenure	Owner, Tenant (social), Tenant (private)
Lone parents employed (2020 only)	n/a

Table A2.4. Official take-up rates for various benefits

Group	Caseload take-up rates			Expenditure take-up rates		
	Income Support or Pension Credit	Housing Benefit	Council Tax Benefit	Income Support or Pension Credit	Housing Benefit	Council Tax Benefit
Lone parents	91.0%	90.0%	86.0%	95.0%	94.0%	90.0%
Couples with children	86.0%	67.0%	54.5%	92.0%	74.5%	60.5%
Working-age people without children	80.5%	82.5%	79.5%	94.5%	87.5%	80.0%
Pensioners[a]	63.0%	85.5%	58.0%	72.5%	90.0%	59.5%

a. Pension Credit is a guaranteed credit for pensioners.
Source: Department for Work and Pensions (2008b).

Table A2.5. Official tax credit take-up rates

Group	Caseload take-up rates		Expenditure take-up rates	
	Child Tax Credit	Working Tax Credit	Child Tax Credit	Working Tax Credit
Working-age people without children	n/a	22%	n/a	28%
Workless families	93%	n/a	95%	n/a
Entitled to both Child and Working Tax Credit	93%	93%	94%	94%
Above Child Tax Credit only threshold, entitled to more than family element	78%	n/a	78%	n/a
Entitled to family element only	71%	n/a	73%	n/a

Source: HM Revenue & Customs (2008).

Table A2.6. Implied caseload take-up rates for various benefits when adjusting for non-take-up (using figures in Table A2.4) and non-reporting of benefit receipt, under the 2010 baseline

Group	Income Support or Pension Credit	Housing Benefit	Council Tax Benefit
Lone parents	79%	67%	65%
Couples with children	67%	50%	42%
Working-age people without children	51%	78%	58%
Pensioners	46%	82%	51%

Source: Authors' calculations using FRS 2005–06 and 2006–07 and assumptions specified in the text.

Table A2.7. Implied caseload take-up rates for tax credits when adjusting for non-take-up (using figures in Table A2.5) and non-reporting of benefit receipt, under the 2010 baseline

Group	Child Tax Credit	Working Tax Credit
Working-age people without children	n/a	16%
Workless families	87%	n/a
Entitled to both Child and Working Tax Credit	91%	91%
Above Child Tax Credit only threshold, entitled to more than family element	74%	n/a
Entitled to family element only	54%	n/a

Source: Authors' calculations using FRS 2005–06 and 2006–07 and assumptions specified in the text.

Table A2.8. Creating the HBAI definition of income from TAXBEN

These are added together:	Gross employment income Gross self-employment income Imputed income from company cars and other benefits in kind Free school meals Savings income Pensions income Income from property Any other unearned income Maintenance payments from absent spouse Benefits
These are subtracted:	Expenses incurred in the course of employment Self-employment net losses Direct taxes Council Tax Contributions to personal pensions Maintenance payments made Parental contributions to students

Appendix 3. Supplementary results

Table A3.1. Forecast child poverty in 2010–11 with no adjustment to the poverty line

Forecast	Before Housing Costs			After Housing Costs		
	Real annual growth in median income, 2006–10 (%)	Relative low income indicator		Real annual growth in median income, 2006–10 (%)	Relative low income indicator	
		Number in poverty (millions)	Child poverty rate (%)		Number in poverty (millions)	Child poverty rate (%)
Central forecast, 2010–11, allowance for non-take-up	0.0	2.1	16.3	0.0	3.3	25.9
Bad recession scenario, 2010–11, allowance for non-take-up	−0.5	2.0	15.9	−0.6	3.3	25.5
Central forecast, 2010–11, allowance for non-take-up and non-reporting	−0.0	2.1	16.6	−0.1	3.4	26.5
Bad recession scenario, 2010–11, allowance for non-take-up and non-reporting	−0.5	2.1	16.2	−0.6	3.4	26.0

Source: Authors' calculations based on FRS 2005–06 and 2006–07 using TAXBEN and assumptions specified in the text.

A3.1 No adjustment to the poverty line

Without the separate non-reporting adjustment, the five policy packages that would reduce child poverty by about 400,000 under the central forecast if they were implemented on top of the baseline are (all financial values are in 2010 prices which, given our assumptions about inflation, are little different to current prices):

1. **Child Tax Credit** only option: Increase the child element of the Child Tax Credit by £420 per year (about £8.08 per week, or a rise of 19%).

2. **Child Benefit** only option: Increase child benefit by £8 per week for all children (a rise of 40% for the first child and 61% for subsequent children).

3. **Child Tax Credit plus large families (CB)**: Increase the child element of the Child Tax Credit by £220 per year (about £4.23 per week, or a 10% rise), and introduce a higher rate of Child Benefit for the third and subsequent children that is £20 per week higher than that of the second child (or 152% higher than Child Benefit would otherwise be for the third and subsequent children).

4. **Child Tax Credit plus large families (CTC)**: Increase the child element of the Child Tax Credit by £275 per year (about £5.29 per week, or a 12% rise), and introduce additional payments for the third and subsequent children paid with the family element of the Child Tax Credit of £20 per week (a 4% increase in the family element for those with three children, or twice that increase for those with four children, etc.). The difference with the above is that the extra support for the third and subsequent children is tapered away from families with incomes over £50,000.

5. **Child Tax Credit plus WTC for couples:** Increase the child element of the Child Tax Credit by £200 per year (about £3.85 per week, or a 9% rise), and increase Working Tax Credit for couples with children by £1,600 per year (£30.77 per week, or a 43% rise).

Table A3.2. Five packages that bring child poverty close to target in 2010 under the central forecast, with costs relative to the central forecast under the policy baseline, with no adjustment to the poverty line

Policy	OECD BHC poverty rate (%)		Cost (£ billion)		Cost per child taken out of poverty (£1,000s)	
	Adjust-ment for non-take-up	Adjust-ment for non-take-up and non-reporting	Adjust-ment for non-take-up	Adjust-ment for non-take-up and non-reporting	Adjust-ment for non-take-up	Adjust-ment for non-take-up and non-reporting
Baseline (central forecast)	16.3	16.6	0	0	0	0
Child Tax Credit option	13.2	13.3	2.7	3.2	6.2	7.6
Child Benefit option	13.2	13.2	5.7	6.7	13	15.8
Child Tax Credit plus large families (CB)	13.3	13.3	3	3.6	7.2	8.4
Child Tax Credit plus large families (CTC)	13.2	13.3	2.9	3.2	6.8	7.6
Child Tax Credit plus higher WTC for couples	13.1	13.2	3.8	5.4	8.4	12.3

Note: All costs relative to the central forecast under the baseline.

Source: Authors' calculations based on FRS 2005–06 and 2006–07 using TAXBEN and various assumptions specified in the text.

Table A3.3 Forecast child poverty in 2020–21, with no adjustment to the poverty line

Lone parent employment assumption	Take-up adjustment	Before Housing Costs			After Housing Costs		
		Real annual growth in median income, 2006–2020 (%)	Children in poverty (millions)	Child poverty rate (%)	Real annual growth in median income, 2006–2020 (%)	Children in poverty (millions)	Child poverty rate (%)
Low	Take-up only	1.2	2.9	21.6	1.1	4.3	31.5
Low	Take-up and non-reporting	1.2	2.9	21.5	1.1	4.3	31.7
Middle	Take-up only	1.2	2.9	21.2	1.1	4.2	31.1
Middle	Take-up and non-reporting	1.2	2.8	21.1	1.1	4.2	31.3
High	Take-up only	1.2	2.8	21.0	1.1	4.2	30.8
High	Take-up and non-reporting	1.2	2.8	20.8	1.1	4.2	30.9

Source: Authors' calculations based on FRS 2005–06 and 2006–07 using TAXBEN and assumptions specified in the text.

When accounting separately for non-reporting in HBAI, the five policy packages that would reduce child poverty by about 400,000 under the central forecast if they were implemented on top of the baseline are (all financial values are in 2010 prices again):

1. **Child Tax Credit** only option: Increase the child element of the Child Tax Credit by £500 per year (about £9.62 per week, or a rise of 22%).

2. **Child Benefit** only option: Increase Child Benefit by £9.50 per week for all children (a rise of 48% for the first child and 72% for subsequent children).

3. **Child Tax Credit plus large families (CB)**: Increase the child element of the Child Tax Credit by £300 per year (about £5.77 per week, or a 13% rise), and introduce a higher rate of Child Benefit for the third and subsequent children that is £20 per week higher than that of the second child (or 152% higher than Child Benefit would otherwise be for the third and subsequent children).

4. **Child Tax Credit plus large families (CTC)**: Increase the child element of the Child Tax Credit by £320 per year (about £6.15 per week, or a 14% rise), and introduce additional payments for the third and subsequent children paid with the family element of the Child Tax Credit of £20 per week (a 4% increase in the family element for those with three children, or twice that increase for those with four children, etc.). The difference with the above is that the extra support for the third and subsequent children is tapered away from families with incomes over £50,000.

5. **Child Tax Credit plus WTC for couples:** Increase the child element of the Child Tax Credit by £300 per year (about £5.77 per week, or a 13% rise), and increase Working Tax Credit for couples with children by £2,100 per year (£40.38 per week, or a 56% rise).

Table A3.4 shows the costs of the three uprating policies between 2010 and 2020 and their effect on child poverty. All financial values are in 2020 prices.

Table A3.4. Hypothetical policy packages for 2020, conditional on implementing the most cost-efficient package for 2010, with no poverty line adjustment

Policy	Employment	BHC poverty rate (%)		Cost (£ billion)	
		Adjust-ment for non-take-up	Adjust-ment for non-take-up and non-reporting	Adjust-ment for non-take-up	Adjust-ment for non-take-up and non-reporting
Baseline (without 2010 package)[19]	Low	21.6	21.5	0.0 (0.0)	0.0 (0.0)
	Middle	21.2	21.1	−0.7 (−0.5)	−0.7 (−0.5)
	High	21.0	20.8	−1.1 (−0.8)	−1.1 (−0.8)
Selective earnings indexation	Low	17.9	16.8	4.6 (3.4)	5.1 (3.8)
	Middle	17.7	16.5	2.2 (1.6)	2.8 (2.0)
	High	17.5	16.3	1.7 (1.3)	2.3 (1.7)
Comprehensive earnings indexation for parents	Low	13.2	13.0	11.0 (8.1)	11.6 (8.5)
	Middle	13.0	12.7	10.3 (7.6)	11.0 (8.1)
	High	12.8	12.5	9.9 (7.3)	10.5 (7.7)
Over-indexation plus higher rate of Working Tax Credit for couples with children	Low	7.2	8.6	25.3 (18.7)	26.3 (19.5)
	Middle	7.1	8.4	24.6 (18.2)	25.6 (18.9)
	High	7.1	8.3	24.1 (17.8)	25.1 (18.6)
Over-indexation plus higher rate of Working Tax Credit for couples with children, with non-take-up of tax credits and benefits halved	Low	5.2	n/a	32.3 (23.9)	n/a
	Middle	5.1	n/a	31.6 (23.3)	n/a
	High	5.0	n/a	31.1 (23.0)	n/a

Source: Authors' calculations based on FRS 2005–06 and 2006–07 using TAXBEN and various assumptions specified in the text.

When we do not adjust the poverty line (upwards), projected child poverty is lower. Therefore, the same uprating policies between 2010 and 2020 result in lower child poverty rates in 2020 when we do not adjust the poverty line. This means that, in order to reduce the child poverty rate to 5% if non-take-up of benefits and tax credits halves, the most expensive package does not need to be quite as generous. Income Support payments for parents and the child element of the Child Tax Credit need to be uprated by 5% per year in real terms between 2010 and 2020, rather than 5.5% per year as is the case when we adjust the poverty line. So the most expensive package is:

---

[19] The increases in the child element of the Child Tax Credit in line with earnings between 2010 and 2020 are not accounted for in the government's public finance projections. If we assumed instead that the child element of the Child Tax Credit would be uprated in line with prices between 2010 and 2020, then, under the middle employment scenario, child poverty in 2020 would be about 500,000 (almost 4 percentage points) higher and the government would spend about £2.5 billion less in current prices.

- **Over-indexation plus higher rate of Working Tax Credit for couples with children:** Uprate all benefits and tax credits for parents in line with earnings, except for Income Support applicable amounts and the child element of the Child Tax Credit, which are uprated by 5% per year in real terms for parents; and introduce a higher rate of Working Tax Credit for couples with children that is 60% higher than the rate for all people with children after this has been earnings-uprated between 2010 and 2020.

2020 costs are presented in current prices, with GDP-adjusted costs in brackets.

References

Adam, S., Brewer, M. and Shephard, A. (2006), *The Trade-Off between Work Incentives and Income Redistribution*. Bristol: The Policy Press.

Berthoud, R., Bryan, M. and Bardasi, E. (2004), *The Dynamics of Deprivation: The Relationship between Income and Material Deprivation over Time*. DWP Research Report 219. Leeds: Corporate Document Services.

Blanden, J., Hansen, K. and Machin, S. (2008), *The GDP Cost of the Lost Earning Potential of Adults who Grew up in Poverty*. York: Joseph Rowntree Foundation.

Brewer, M., Browne, K. and Sutherland, H. (2006), *Micro-simulating Child Poverty in 2010 and 2020*. York: Joseph Rowntree Foundation.

Brewer, M., Goodman, A. and Leicester, A. (2006), *Household Spending in Britain: What Can it Teach us about Poverty?* Bristol: The Policy Press.

Brewer, M., Goodman, A., Shaw, J. and Shephard, A. (2005), *Poverty and Inequality in Britain: 2005*. IFS Commentary 99. London: Institute for Fiscal Studies.

Brewer, M., Goodman, A, Shaw, J. and Sibieta, L. (2006), *Poverty and Inequality in Britain: 2006*. IFS Commentary 101. London: Institute for Fiscal Studies, **doi**: 10.1920/co.ifs.2006.0101.

Brewer, M., Muriel, A., Phillips, D. and Sibieta, L. (2008), *Poverty and Inequality in the UK: 2008*. London: Institute for Fiscal Studies.

Brewer, M., Ratcliffe, A. and Smith, S. (2008), 'Does welfare reform affect fertility? Evidence from the UK', IFS Working Paper 08/09, **doi**: 10.1920/wp.ifs.2007.0809.

Brewer, M., Saez, E. and Shephard, A. (2009, forthcoming), 'Means-testing and tax rates on earnings', in J. Mirrlees, S. Adam, T. Besley, R. Blundell, S. Bond, R. Chote, M. Gammie, P. Johnson, G. Myles and J. Poterba (eds), *Dimensions of Tax Design: The Mirrlees Review*. Oxford: Oxford University Press for Institute for Fiscal Studies (www.ifs.org.uk/mirrlees/mrPublications).

Child Poverty Unit (2009), *Ending Child Poverty: Making It Happen*. London: CPU.

Department for Work and Pensions (2003), *Measuring Child Poverty*. London: DWP.

Department for Work and Pensions (2005), *The New Family Resources Survey Grossing Regime* (http://www.dwp.gov.uk/asd/frs/reports/new_grossing_regime.pdf).

Department for Work and Pensions (2008a), *Households below Average Income 1994/95–2006/07*. Leeds: Corporate Document Services.

Department for Work and Pensions (2008b), *Income Related Benefits: Estimates of Take Up in 2006–07* (http://www.dwp.gov.uk/asd/income_analysis/jun_2008/0607_Publication.pdf).

Giles, C. and McCrae, J. (1995), *TAXBEN: The IFS Micro-simulation Tax and Benefit Model*. IFS Working Paper W95/19.

Gregg, P., Harkness, S. and MacMillan, L. (2006), *Welfare to Work Policies and Child Poverty*. York: Joseph Rowntree Foundation.

Hirsch, D. (2006), *What Will it Take to End Child Poverty?* York: Joseph Rowntree Foundation.

HM Revenue & Customs (2008), *Child Tax Credit and Working Tax Credit Take-Up Rates, 2005–06* (http://www.hmrc.gov.uk/stats/personal-tax-credits/cwtc-take-up2005-06.pdf).

HM Treasury (2007a), *Pre-Budget Report, November 2007* (http://www.hm-treasury.gov.uk/bud_budget07_repindex.htm).

HM Treasury (2007b), *PSA Delivery Agreement 9: Halve the Number of Children in Poverty by 2010–11, on the Way to Eradicating Child Poverty by 2020*. London: The Stationery Office (http://hm-treasury.gov.uk/cmselect/cmworpen/42/4202.htm).

HM Treasury (2008), *Pre-Budget Report, November 2008* (https://www.hm-treasury.gov.uk/prebud_pbr08_index.htm).

House of Commons Treasury Committee (2008), *The 2008 Budget*. HC 430. London: The Stationery Office.

Machin, S. and McNally, S. (2006), *Education and Child Poverty*. York: Joseph Rowntree Foundation (http://www.jrf.org.uk/publications/education-and-child-poverty-literature-review).

Parsons, J. and Rees, P. with Norman, P., Boden, P. and Wohland, P. (2008), *Child Poverty in the UK: Socio-demographic Scenarios to 2020 for Children (2008 update). Report on Datasets, Models and Results*. Mimeograph, University of Leeds.